Love Letters from Mother Nature

Shelley Neller grew up in Dayboro, Queensland. She did her journalism cadetship with Queensland Newspapers, Brisbane. In 1975-76 she worked in News Limited's London bureau, before moving to Sydney where she worked for several newspapers including *The Australian*, *The Daily Telegraph* and *Sunday Telegraph*. As a freelancer, her writing has appeared in *The National Times*, *The Bulletin* and various national magazines. In 1984 she established her own public relations company which served a broad corporate clientele. She has co-written three non-fiction books (*Set Yourself Free*, *Free to Be Me* and *The Home Show*) and edited several others. In 1992 she relocated to Byron Bay.

Love Letters from Mother Nature

A meditative journey

SHELLEY NELLER

First published by Bruce Sims Books, 2000
68 Abbotsford Street, Abbotsford Vic 3067
brucesims@bigpond.com

Designed by Helen Semmler
Typeset in Palatino and Cushing Book by Midland Typesetters, Maryborough, Victoria
Printed and bound in Australia by Australian Print Group, Maryborough, Victoria

National Library of Australia
Cataloguing-in-Publication data

Neller, Shelley.
Love letters from Mother Nature.

Bibliography.
ISBN 0 9577800 2 8.

1. Self-perception. 2. Spirituality. 3. Nature –
Psychological aspects. I. Title.

291.4

5 4 3 2 1

Distributed by Australian Book Group, 03 5625 4290, Fax 03 5625 3756

A c k n o w l e d g m e n t s

There is not enough space here to thank the many people, places, plants and creatures, who wittingly or unwittingly shapeshifted themselves into the cosmic contours of Mother Nature and thereby contributed to my writing this book. When it comes to itemising gratitude, the universe is a pretty daunting rollcall.

But thanks have to start somewhere, so I'll begin with my agent, Sheila Drummond, for her belief in my work, her inclusivity and her persistence; and my publisher, Bruce Sims, who recognises the existence of the 'alternative majority' and understands that any of us can journey to other dimensions.

My appreciation goes to Elizabeth Lamond, who 'saw' the cover years before I did; to Bubula Lardi, who helped me to get off the merry-go-round for long enough to begin to hear the voices; to Lesley Meredith for plant talk, plain talk and helpful remedies; and to Penelope Ward, who helped to speed things along.

For their sisterly love, laughter and unstinting support, let me also thank Lizi Beadman, Jenny Bird, Kate Stead, Susie Shepherd, Julie Stanton and Annie Wright. And for permission to include their personal writings, I express additional appreciation to Susie Shepherd and Catriona. Merci to Rod Gibson for his gift of 'Coastal Dreaming'. For their brotherly love and encouragement, I thank Aaron Beth'el and Michael Hawton.

Ian Greenhalgh, Janice Rogers and Pat Cranz from the Byron Bay Library joined in my spirit of exploration and sleuthed the most obscure requests.

Harry Moult and Peter Parker helped confirm a number of flora and fauna references, but the responsibility for any errors is mine.

Gratitude to Reyna Matthes for serendipitous connections and to Tracylee Arestides for her gentle pep-talks and creative PR input.

Thanks to my parents, Deirdre and Bill, and my sisters, Gay and Tracey, for their love, prayers, humour and shelter; and to my late grandparents – Arthur, who introduced me to gardening and the fruits which that can bear; Bertha, who encouraged me to pay attention to dreams and affirmed my childhood belief in other realities; and Maisie, whose beloved greenhouses showed me that nature can bloom and nurture us, even in very small spaces.

Permission to quote Mandawuy Yunupingu's lyrics from 'Tribal Voice' and 'My Kind of Life' was gratefully received from Mushroom Music Publishing; Van Morrison's lyrics from 'Days Like This' © copyright 1994 Exile Publishing Ltd/ Universal Music Publishing Pty Ltd, are reproduced by kind permission of Universal Publishing Group; permission to quote Audre Lorde's essay 'Uses of the Erotic: The Erotic as Power' was gratefully received from The Crossing Press, Inc., Freedom, California.

Contents

1 A Thousand Cobwebs ...   1

2 The Call   10

3 The Gardens   15

4 Setting Out   22

5 Encountering Nature   26

6 Developing Ears   30

7 A Wing and a Prayer   36

8 Wild Spirit   45

9 Wanganui   53

10 The Grand Design   62

11 Waiting for Sunshine   71

12 Where the Garden Takes You   79

13 Cultivating Mystery and Trust   84

14 Meeting a Monarch   94

15 Under the Canopy   101

16 Light Moves   103

17 Moonshadow   111

18 Ex Libris   120

19 Clear Sailing and Shipwreck   132

20 The Blessing of Beauty   150

21 Songlines   158

22 Embracing the Erotic   167

23 The Dance of the Fireflies   186

24 Assorted Armageddons   196

25 Rising and Returning   207

26 The Rainbow Season   221

27 Tribal Voices   231

28 Reflections   244

Recommended reading   265

'... all that I know speaks to me through this earth and
I long to tell you, you who are earth, too and *listen as we
speak to each other of what we know: the light is in us.'*
SUSAN GRIFFIN

ON THE EIGHTH DAY, GOD CREATED BYRON BAY –
BUMPER STICKER

1

A Thousand Cobwebs ...

We positioned ourselves around the big boardroom table. Six senior executives and me. In our suits.

My client, a sanguine, snowy-bearded King Neptune character, sat on my left. On my right, his jittery marketing manager drummed his chewed fingertips on the shiny felled cedar. Four admen flanked the far rim of the table. One leaned back in his big black swivel chair, legs splayed; another cupped his hands behind his head, elbows akimbo. The third hunched over the table, doodling on scrap paper. The fourth stared out the windows to the panoramic views of the harbour and the bridge. The admen, in their forties, looked jaded. They also looked mad as hell, as if they weren't going to take it anymore.

King Neptune's high-profile enterprise had hit a serious cash flow problem and the agency's payment for 'creative input' was overdue. Neptune had brought a cheque to the meeting, but the admen were not mollified. The boardroom reeked of the threat of an altercation. What kind of week or life the admen were having was anyone's guess, but I could sense they wanted more than payment. They wanted blood.

Polite exchanges swiftly gave way to shouting, to an hour of the gladiatorial, expletive-undeleted raging that can pass for a civilised business meeting in this country. It made my stomach churn. At a pivotal point in this hostile scene, a skein of seven white ibis winged past us, seven corporate specimens under glass.

Neptune turned to me. 'What should we tell the media, if anything?' he asked, but I found myself momentarily unable to reply because the ibis had somehow lodged a wishbone in my throat. The birds had stalked me with the notion (not a new one) that it might be possible to live another way, in another place ...

After the meeting, armed with a fresh working brief, I hastened, past the high-rises and into the street tunnel to catch a train back to my downtown office. Halfway through the tunnel, unaccountably, I looked up. There, in a hairline crack in the peak of the cement arch, a maidenhair fern was growing, like a fine-branched stalactite, down towards the light. The sheer valour and genius of that endeavour stalked me, too.

As I squeezed into a carriage packed with dozens of other 'thinking termites' dressed as formally and funereally as myself, I gripped a standing pole. I had begun work at 7.30am, stopped only to gulp a sandwich at noon, and now felt drained from the bludgeoning tactics of the boys in the boardroom. I had urgent work to do for another client who wanted a major media launch organised 'yesterday'. The checklist ran: compile invitation lists, write press releases and speeches, art direct photographs of the new product, get invitations designed and printed, book venues, arrange catering, brief and delegate tasks to my staff.

Almost certainly my secretary would greet me with about

a dozen phone messages from clients and journalists, all requiring prompt responses. Plus I was late preparing the monthly client reports and invoices. If they weren't mailed in the next day or so, I'd have my own cash flow crisis to contend with.

What to do? What to do first? What time would I finally get out of the office? It didn't bear thinking about. My head spun. I sighed, then pinched my cheeks to try to perk myself up, to ward against feeling sucked, body and scoured soul, into The Vortex. As the train rolled over the bridge, clackety-clack, clackety-clack, I silently incanted 'means-to-an-end, means-to-an-end', my five o'clock vespers. But when that 'end' might arrive, I could not speculate. I could not think beyond the demands of today, lest the mere effort leach the life force out of me.

*   *   *

It was an Indian summer. Up at the Cross, the steam rose from the footpaths. The cafe was the latest in radiology chic, all steel and starkness, uneased by a single soft furnishing or flower. The waiter had city-gym biceps and spiky, artfully dyed and jelled yellow hair with black roots. In order to be heard above the clang of the kitchen, the din of the diners, the full-blast sporting commentary on the television, the blare of Eric Clapton on the CD player, and the passing traffic, my friend and I yelled for coffee and focaccia.

While we waited, two carloads of police with guns and a white van carrying two burly men in black trousers and white shirts pulled up outside a seedy boarding house nearby.

'They'll go in and come out with a body,' I predicted.

'How can you tell?' asked my friend, who was the only

other diner paying attention to what was probably a common-place sight in this area.

'Those guys in the white shirts are from the morgue, not the ambulance.'

The men walked into the building and my friend and I got down to tintacks. We intended to jointly pitch for several new accounts and we needed to discuss strategies, ideas, fees. Deadlines (or 'deadloins' as we jokingly referred to them because of the effect they had on our love lives) were looming. We would divvy up the business proposals and write them over the weekend. There was no time to do this during normal office hours, of course. Like most of our contemporaries, our Monday-to-Friday schedules were already crammed to capacity.

Between taking calls on her mobile phone (I had stalwartly refused to buy one), my colleague showed me some background information about a potential account in which mention was made of two penguins, each of whom, while swimming in public waterways, had lost a wing to power boat propellers. The penguins, fortunately, had been rescued and healed. As I read and re-read the details about the penguins, tears slid down my cheeks. My colleague, embarrassed by this public display of emotion, tried to soothe me. 'Don't cry,' she said. 'It'll be an easy sell. The TV crews will love them.'

The morgue men emerged from the boarding house, bearing a stretcher with a body covered by a white sheet. No one batted an eyelid.

* * *

Step on the gas, I urged myself, clicking on my right indicator as I approached that section of the road where the left lane was required to merge with the right. 'Merge' as anyone who has driven amongst Sydney's ill-mannered motorists knows, is a euphemism for push, butt, nip or cut in as soon as a margin of space between bumper bars is visible. If you wait for a gracious driver to decelerate even for the few seconds it takes to permit you to 'merge' in front of him or her, you could end up waiting for Godot. A quick glance in the rear vision mirror revealed a healthy margin of space between me and a new black BMW convertible. I accelerated in plenty of time, steered right, and I was in. All fair and legal road etiquette.

Seconds later, I stopped at a red light. An explosion of noise made me look left. Beside me in a newly formed left lane, was the BMW. Its occupants, two young bare-chested men sporting fashionably stubbled faces and baseball caps worn backwards, were screaming at me above the top volume of their radio. The passenger gave me the finger. The driver's jaws were wrenched asunder in a rictus of rage.

'Fuckin' bitch!' he bellowed. And worse. Saliva sprayed from his cavernous mouth. Two decades of living in big cities and still I was not up to this kind of attack. I turned away, looked straight ahead, longed for the lights to change. I became aware that my teeth were clenched and I was barely breathing, so I inhaled deeply, deliberately, taking the breath down to the tightness in my chest, then slowly releasing it. Until the green light flashed. And I was off.

*   *   *

I went to pitch for new business with clients who turned out to be charming. However, after two hours of discussion, it was obvious they were covertly trying to milk all my creative ideas with no intention of showing the colour of their money.

Them's the breaks, I told myself as I drove away. Impetuously, I decided to take a slight detour to the Baha'i Temple for ten stolen minutes of quiet time, a quick and guilty pleasure amidst the foolscap sheets of my 'To Do' lists.

As I pulled out of the temple's driveway on to the busy main road, I noticed a snowy white cat lying dead on the shoulder of the road. It was cold and stiff as I lifted and placed it carefully under a shrub outside the only nearby house. No one was home so I set off for my next appointment, saying prayers for the spirit of Snowy, as I called him.

The next evening, en route to an obligatory dinner in a leafy beachside suburb, I turned up a side street and swerved to miss another cat, also apparently dead, on the road. I stopped the car to take a closer look. The big old tabby was warm, newly killed, lying in a spreading pool of blood. A few metres away, four teenagers in boardshorts, obviously locals, were discussing which film they proposed to see at the cinema that evening.

'Excuse me. Do you live in this street?' I asked.

'Yeah,' said the spokesman.

'Did you notice the dead cat?'

'Yeah.'

'Do you know whose it is?'

'Nuh.'

'Would you have a shovel I could borrow to lift the cat off the road?'

Silence. Blank looks. As I turned away, they immediately resumed their movie discussion.

'Do you have a cat?' I asked the woman in the nearest house, dreading she would say yes.

'I have three,' she replied.

'Are they all here?'

'They're curled up in front of the heater.'

Relieved, I told her about the dead tabby. She took a shovel from her garage, I took an old towel from the boot of my car and together we gently removed the slain creature to her backyard where, she assured me, she would give it a decent burial and then try to locate its owners.

I arrived at the dinner distressed. My companions were engaged in that quintessential late twentieth century Sydney ritual of sharing their traffic experiences – which roads they'd taken or avoided, how badly banked up the traffic had been, the maniacs they'd encountered on the freeway, how long it had taken them to get there. Only when the Sydney Traffic Demon had been exorcised collectively could talk move on to more significant matters, such as real estate.

One woman fumbled in her handbag and pulled out not a mobile phone but a calculator. With a few deft sums, The Calculator tallied up for the man beside her the monthly repayments on an interest-only home loan, the depreciation allowance claimable and the total annual tax benefits of investing in a brand new duplex somewhere in an upwardly mobile suburb.

The man asked her about capital gains tax and she pushed a few more buttons.

I pushed the penne arabiata around my plate.

'Cheer up,' said the Calculator's husband, as he nudged me with a bottle of beaujolais. 'It was only a cat and there's plenty more where that one came from.'

* * *

I was relaxing at home with Metropolitan Man, listening generously to his ideas for new ventures, his struggles to find good staff, the right commercial location. He asked whether I thought he had engaged the most efficient media monitoring service. They had failed to clip a mention of him in a business magazine recently. Meanwhile, a story about one of his new financial escapades, inexplicably had not appeared in the city's paper of record.

'You must be wondering if you still exist,' I teased.

'I know I do when I sign the cheques,' he retorted. And so it went, the banter of familiars.

Over dinner, I steered our conversational canoe into broader waters. This Metropolitan Man was a nature lover, of sorts, and recently I had read an interesting view of humanity's relationship to nature.

'Wanna hear it?'

' 'way you go,' he said, his turn to indulge my interests.

I fetched the book and read:

'... as a species ... you have considered yourselves as apart from the rest of nature and consciousness.

'Your own survival as a species was your main concern. You considered other species only in the light of their use to you. You did not have any true conception of the great sacredness of all consciousness, nor of your relationship with it. You were losing your grasp of that great truth.

'In the present circumstances you are carrying that idea forward – of species survival regardless of the consequences, the idea of changing the environment to suit your own purposes; and this has led you to a disregard of spiritual truths.

'In physical reality, therefore, you are seeing the results . . .'

'And where does the sheila who wrote this live?'

'It's not exactly written by a woman.'

'Well, the bloke, then?'

'It's not exactly a bloke, either.'

He raised his eyebrows.

'It's an energy personality essence,' I ventured.

He yawned. It was only eight-thirty, but empire-building can leave you too enervated to entertain esoterica after dinner.

'From another dimension,' I added.

'Yeah, yeah,' he said wearily, 'but what I want to know is: where's the rub?'

'The rub?'

'You know,' he answered, rubbing his thumb against his fingers, 'where do you send your twenty five bucks for the information?'

And so it went, until lights out.

'What are you thinking?' Metro Man whispered in my ear as he wrapped his arms around me.

I was thinking: I want to set off for somewhere quiet and green and beautiful, and when I get there I want to fall down on the warm earth and swoon, slack-jawed, under the spell of the sensuous.

'I'm thinking,' I told him, 'that life's a pitch, and then you die.'

* * *

Amid the daily hubbub, these were not memorialising moments, but over the years they did accrue. As the Indians say, a thousand cobwebs can trap a tiger.

2

The Call

And so, paradoxically, for a long time before I quit the city, I felt not only ensnared by my environment, but also oddly disconnected from it, a detached observer of the peculiarities of the urban jungle. On the rare occasions when I went downtown, I encountered a sea of strained, blank or downcast faces, avoiding eye contact as they scurried along.

I noticed that my fellow city-dwellers did not take their observations from nature or the seasons; they took them from television and talkback radio. I fretted that I, too, had lost the ability to relate to the natural world. One sultry February night, I watched a paper moon rise above the clustered skyscrapers and it looked artificial to me, like a chimera or a special effect from one of the film sets I'd worked on.

That night I dreamed I was in a department store, but uninterested in any of the merchandise. The lights dimmed and a beautiful woman handed me two ripe avocados, saying, 'Your mother found these on the moon and asked me to give them to you. If you hold one in each hand, you can fly to wherever you want.' I took the avocados and began to run. My body lifted up to the lofty ceiling, from where I gazed dispassionately at the displayed goods, the milling people. I decided to try flying outside. It was a sunny day and I flew over a wide green meadow dotted with trees. The air currents spoke to me. 'Come with us,' they called. They sounded whimsical, mischievous. In their midst, I flew higher and higher, enjoying the freedom of gliding and soaring with them, until dusk when it was time to descend. I landed in a lush walled garden and found myself naked. I knelt down on the earth. In my hands the avocados had turned into two golden orbs, which I carefully laid at the base of a fishtail palm.

With hindsight, I see in this dream multiple layers of the unconscious at play – its archetypal artistry, its potent prescience, its glossary of living wisdom – but that morning when I woke up and noted it down, I simply said to myself: Well, chickadee, looks like you're getting ready to fly the coop.

Which came as no surprise. By then I already had downsized from a CBD office and several staff to sole trading from my spare bedroom.

The air was as thick as the Harbour Bridge traffic at peak hour; all around the apartment was the relentless rumble of urban logos. While I shuffled papers on my desk, the computer hummed its own fast, foreign language, fat with formats, fonts and figures of speech, but unable, finally, to speak to me or soothe the scrape of isolation inside my skin. I stared at the blank screen and my eyes glazed over. For the umpteenth time that morning I looked at my watch and felt my life arrowed, carved up, accounted for and charged out in quarter-hour segments. I had twenty minutes to get to a business appointment across town, an unlikely achievement considering the traffic and the paucity of parking spaces.

And when I got there, would I be able, one more time, to

muster the requisite charm and concern, to write like a fast hired gun about whomever or whatever it was they wished to promote to the great unwashed masses? If I could feel an empathy for them, I would. But meanwhile, time ticked by with agonising slowness and my efficacy in this quick-or-dead commercial bullring began to render me numb. I was starting to feel like a tired and remorseful matador who wished to fling away the red cape, to abandon the whole herd of big business bulls to their own devices in that crowded city arena and nip off for a long respite on some palm-fringed costa.

Client copy and, with it, a fair-sized cheque was due any day, but I was restless. Not just fidgety or momentarily discombobulated by the heat, but terribly hollow, swamped by a deep accidie.

Adhering to the puritan work ethic of my culture and my times, I had tried for years to slough off any sense of personal isolation by labouring dedicatedly to create meaning and find self-worth – setting specific goals, striving to achieve them, doing certain deeds. For so many years I had been a high chaparral of activity, accomplishment and acquisition, yet fulfilment somehow remained an elusive riddle. Despite the typical chockablock diary of the urban-dweller who lives life allegro, it all felt like a dress rehearsal for ... for what? For the fanfare of real life to begin?

I paced about, ending up in my bedroom. I rested my arms on the sill of the open window and looked into the green heart of the liquidambar tree whose branches and leaves brushed against the wall of the building. Its broad, dense canopy shielded me from the intense eastern sun.

Silently I spoke to the tree: I feel empty and isolated and I'm tired of trying to do better. What does 'do better' mean,

anyhow? More antiques? More Sydney rock oysters, more
software, more silk dresses, more harbour views, more pages
in my curriculum vitae? I don't understand – there must be
more. Please give me a sign.

I closed my eyes and waited. After a few minutes, my
scrambled, anxious thoughts began to settle, and dissolve,
and then I heard a reply in a voice that was distinctly female.
She said:

If you want to understand the nature of things, first
you need to understand some things about Nature.

It was a genial, still voice, yet it had the authority of a woman
who would not hesitate to make rogue waves, if she deemed
it necessary. Like a ship becalmed on a flat, glassy sea, a
vessel going nowhere, I felt the echoes of that female voice
rippling within me and feared it had the impulsion to carry
me far from the conventional ambition which had served me
since childhood; to catapult me into the depths of that wild
waterway, the Unknown.

When I opened my eyes, I saw a small white feather, half
the length of my little finger, drifting down. I could not see
or hear a bird, but that does not mean there was not one very
near, for those canny creatures are masters of camouflage. I
caught the feather in the warm bowl of my outstretched palms
and cradled it like a precious augury from invisible allies. If
I had possessed more knowledge, I probably could have
identified the bird, or even its age and gender from that lone
feather. But in that moment all I knew was that for such a
light object with no extrinsic worth, it weighed in with
substantial solace and significance.

It would have been easy to cite the traffic, the pollution,

the pace, the spiralling cost of living or any one of the blemishes and bruises of city life for my eventual departure. But ultimately the leave-taking was not a reaction against those flaws. It was an ineluctable tug towards something else. While those detractions irritated me, chipping away at my long-time affinity with the place, there was a parallel force of inner attrition at work, an incisive hunger which gnawed at my sense of well-being the longer I tarried.

I had unquestionably heard Her voice, and even if She was only one of the colourful troop of sub-personalities we all have corralled in our psyches, it was apparent She was one in need of attention, a compelling one with something to say. If I ignored Her, the consequences would be upon my own head or heart.

I carried the feather back to my desk and tried to resume my work, but procrastination (the practical kind has always been my speciality) overtook me. I got up several times – to swallow vitamins, to take out the garbage, to clean the bath, to check the mailbox.

At my desk again, I tapped on the keyboard with my pen for several minutes, then tossed it in the air.

'That's it!' I announced out loud to myself and the feather. I checked the phone book and began to dial an inner-city number.

As I punched the numbers in, I thought about desire and how, unlike obligation, it has no blueprint, no measured white lines of tomorrow traced on today's blue background. You can spontaneously sketch in some faint, new lines and directions as they present themselves, but finally, you just have to follow the insistent voices of your dreams, I concluded, as the phone started ringing at the other end.

3

____

The Gardens

After a roundrobin of transfers through the Royal Botanic
Gardens' bureaucracy, I finally got through to a good-
humoured and charitable woman, who was sympathetic to my
left-brain burnout, my concern about disappearing up my own
spellcheck, and my pressing need to stick my hands in the
dirt. The Gardens had no scheme for volunteer gardeners,
she explained[1], but she would speak to the leading hand.
Bless her, she must have persuaded him of my enthusiasm,
for my credentials (childhood helpmeet in my grandfather's
vegetable patch) were a bit light on.

'We've never had a volunteer before, so we'll start you in
the rose garden and see how you go,' he said kindly on my
first day. One of his staff showed me the correct way to prune,
then left me to it. Sedulously, I clipped those blooms on the
turn from full to fading, then tossed them into a wheelbarrow.
There were rows upon rows of them and, for the first half-
hour or so, I tried to calculate when I'd get to the end of
them all. Fortunately, it was so hot that I gave up that goal-
oriented attitude and allowed myself to become lost in the
steady clip-and-toss of the work. An intense layer of heat

swarmed up from the baking soil and made my whole body sweat, but I didn't mind.

The low-decibel buzz of the city traffic was all around me, whizzing along the expressway and down the wind-whipped streets between the high rises. Marooned on that quiet island of beauty and tranquillity, I enjoyed it as a pleasant, if surreal juxtaposition. Time lost its sharp, pressing edges and, as I pruned at my own pace, my mind took a break from its usual schematic bent. For so long my creative and spiritual needs had been hidden in the thick grey, 'secure' forest of economic scaffolding or sacrificed on the secular altar of organisation that they had become etiolated, withered and almost lost to me.

For years, I had focussed so intently on *how* to be more efficient in my work that I'd forgotten *why* I was doing it, let alone *where* my contribution fitted into any larger scheme. All at once, the roses' scent struck the ding of memory, of a birthday gift a lover had once given me – four dozen red roses that actually smelled real and a T-shirt that said: 'I know I'm efficient. Tell me I'm beautiful.' For his birthday, I'd reciprocated sentimentally and aphoristically with a pair of roller skates and a T-shirt that read: 'Kiss me now – I have to get on with my career.' Which he treasured and jogged in till it rotted ...

Through the day, all sorts of people approached me. 'Nice job you've got there.' 'Aren't you the lucky one?' And so on. Two rosarians, a retired Canadian couple on holiday, outlined the idiosyncratic growing habits of the Mister Lincoln rose. It was all beyond my ken, but I smiled at this received wisdom because I could see they were just parlaying anecdotes to make contact, to say how beautiful they found the harbour and how much they loved their own garden in Toronto. If you had to be plugged into a worldwide web, as everyone kept insisting, then this was a pretty folksy network.

At lunchtime, I sprawled under a massive weeping fig, ate a sandwich and squinted through dark glasses at the lapping harbour waters suffused with light. The high noon rays bouncing off the salt water were so blinding that I had to rest my retinas every few minutes by looking down at my feet, at the shaded sphere of lawn.

Scientists, so I'd read, could measure the light that entered my eyes; they could measure the pulses that went deep into my brain from the retina, but they could not pinpoint, could not capture the nanosecond when that became a visual perception. What I saw, ultimately, was still a mystery to them. How much more of a mystery then was the sublime, yet nebulous, desideratum I felt when I looked into that intense spectrum, one that dug into me and at the same time reached out towards that endless light. I longed to lose myself in it, to have it confer on me an epiphany perhaps, or a blessing ... Yet if I reeled in my attention and breathed, I could already feel a blessing within the finitude of my body as I ate the bread, as I gave weight to the earth, as my slight sun-warmed torso sank gratefully into that green pile. 'Serious science' might relegate me to the lower ranks of mere corporeality, a piece of dense matter which, like all matter, is said to have 'tendencies to exist', but scientific studies seemed so remote from and unrelated to my own life experience.

As late as the 1990s, it was pronounced peremptorily that 'science is, simply, what is known, and the only alternative to it is ignorance'. In my ignorant (the pronouncers would say 'female') way of trying to see both sides, I gave thanks for the fact that science, through technology, had in many ways liberated the lives of my generation. I did not wish to demonise science, to denigrate 'Mathematical Man' and the Holy Rollers of the New Physics, the high priests of meaningless matter, the unlockers of the 'Mind of God' and all that ... Yet, it struck me that, despite their generally good intentions, the scientists, swimming around in their limited and assumed realities like fish unaware they're in water, left a lot out of their investigations and equations. Also, I could not overlook the extent of science's destructively masculine drives in the macrocosm. The cold light of pure reason casts its own long shadow. And I'd heard tell, too, that Voltaire, that hubristic grand-daddy of rationalism, spent his old age with a priest at his side.

In my somewhat disenchanted microcosm, I saw my own masculine drives running rampant. And I understood, intellectually, the Jungian principle that she who rides her animus[2] like a wild bronco for decades will eventually have a bad fall. But in those days, although I craved fundamental change, for me to cut my umbilical ties to haste and activity, to talk and noise, to surrender to the 'loss of self, sacrifice, inner transformation and change' that true spiritual life is about, was beyond my capacity. Yoga and daily meditations notwithstanding, I was still too swept up in the momentous power and thrill of the ride, too fiercely and fearfully tunnel-visioned to entertain, let alone attempt another approach to life, another *via* not only to survive, but to flourish ...

Two stylishly-dressed young women approached and sat nearby and pretty soon our collective attention was drawn to a handsome Australian wood duck waddling past a bed of blush-tinted canna lillies near the water's edge. The bird's casual strides were underlined by his short, nasally 'gnow, gnow's?'

'Isn't it gorgeous?' one woman addressed the other.

'Love those stripey feathers,' replied the second. 'Very Laura Ashley.'

'More Country Road, don't you think?'

By day's end I'd made half a dozen trips to the compost heap to empty from my barrow the cuttings of cream, blood red, apricot, primrose and lilac blooms. After I'd returned my gloves and implements to their storage places, I set out for my bus stop. One of the gardeners intercepted me with a large bunch of mixed roses wrapped in newspaper.

'It's against the rules,' he shrugged, 'but ...'

'Thanks, they're beautiful,' I replied. And went home gladly weary.

On the bus a thirtysomething woman in basic black (de rigueur downtown clobber) with a glossy clutch of designer-label shopping bags sat next to me. In a weekend newspaper once, I'd read that 'while few of us can identify six species of birds or local flora, the average adult can recognise about one thousand logos or labels'. Despite the expensive booty balanced on her tailored skirt, she looked tense and glum. In the past I had indulged in a fair share of retail therapy myself. The consolatory beauty of luxury items in particular had helped to take the edge off whatever was bothering me in my current reality. But it was always a quick, temporary fix, a second prize for I knew not what. Part of life's journey seemed to entail unknotting the tightly convoluted connections between what you thought you wanted and what you really wanted, or, more pertinently, needed. And that could take some time, a commodity which traded at a premium in the city.

I stretched out my legs and, intermittently sniffing my own cache of beautiful, gratuitous contraband, watched the urban world go by – the brisk, resolute strides of those on the footpaths, the slow crawling traffic, the bumper stickers that said: SHIT HAPPENS!

Riding on that bus, I worried that time was marching on and that despite my jam-packed, hasty lifestyle, I was dragging the chain in my own evolution. Like a zero-time particle, my very existence was in question. Time, I've since learned, does not march on. *We* march on at the speed of light in time, that 'imaginary dimension of space', even while we're sitting still. And zero-time particles apparently do exist – as light particles, the very light we see with our eyes and which physicists call photons.

Photons, it turns out, don't spend any time in our world (or maybe in any other world for that matter). So here we encounter 'mysticism supported by physics on a grand scale'. According to physicist Fred Wolf, 'light, like a disinterested sculptor, spends no time in the universe that it created.' For light, Wolf explains, 'birth and death are one. This property of zero-time particles makes photons exist on a borderline between solid, tangible and the ethereal, potential'. This concept, had I known of it then, would have held a particular significance for me as I was straddling a similar borderline.

Over the months, I did various jobs at the Gardens. One day, I was assigned to tidy up the succulent beds, and although I avoided being jabbed by the large cacti prickles, dozens of the small almost invisible ones had insidiously penetrated my gloves. It took days to extract them all. Death by a thousand cuts, I thought, while riding home in a jam-packed blue bus. Metaphor appealed to me because it seemed to inject a kind of vitality into the quotidian, to liberate me from the flat-earth reality of my own pedestrian plotline.

Still, it was important to know when to take things literally and when to act. To me, the cultivating of a garden promised a certain raw vigour, a directness of experience that by-passed the distractive pyrotechnics of language and cut straight to the heart and soul. There seemed no doubt that a garden possessed the power to heal and restore.

In due course, however, I felt so out of synch with city life, so charged with the unequivocal completion of that long life cycle, that no amount of power-walking through garden suburbs, 'getaway' weekends in rustic settings, not even those therapeutic stints in the Gardens, appeased the clamouring to cut loose and move on. When a 'sea-change into something rich and strange' is at hand, the best thing to do is to swim with it. And so, holding the image of a garden as a mindful focal point (and not, I hoped, a mirage) I packed up and travelled north.

About that adventurous quantum leap I have some stories to tell, but they are not entirely my own, as you will see.

1. A few years after my experience, the Friends of the Royal Botanic Gardens, Sydney, introduced 'Helping Hands', which is a privilege for its members to assist the horticulturists once a month with labour-saving tasks such as mulching, dead-heading and weeding.
2. The masculine principle present in the female unconscious.

4

Setting Out

It was evening and I was tired when my car crested the big hill soon after Possum Creek. A providential flash of light crossed crossed my face, then rapidly swept the landscape ahead, and I let out a whoop of joy.

'Lighthouse: A fixed structure in the form of a tower equipped with a light visible to mariners for warning them of obstructions, for making harbour entrances.'

Despite the dismantling of the formerly fixed structures of my life and despite my impecunious state and indeterminate direction, what I trusted in that moment was a gut feeling that I was entering a sheltered port. It might contain dangerous swells from time to time. There might be hidden shoals and violent, electrical storms. But as I turned off the highway, none of this mattered to me. I did not pretend to know where life was leading. I was on a voyage of trust. I felt nervous, yet as light and vibrant as a fluorescent buoy.

Having lived in various places on the planet, I'd learned that the grass was not greener elsewhere, it was greener where you watered it. I didn't believe in place as panacea. Surely life in this neck of the woods, or what's left of them, would be, like everywhere else, crowded with cautionary tales for all its inhabitants. The narrative of my life, like most people's, had had its fair share of bathos, so I was not anticipating double rainbows in my back yard or positive vibrations up my kundalini, although, in due course, I would get to revel in the rapture of both. Still, it would be untrue to deny that I hoped for some undefined reward for my willingness to make changes in latitude and attitude – even if that reward was only the self-energising virtue of having taken the risk and made the shift.

I grew up in a generation which has thrived on the freedom to pick and choose who or what to follow, believe in, experiment with. I can subscribe, or not, to dogmas of my own choice. I can take or leave crystals, tantra, astrology, rebirthing, spiritual healing, channelling and all the rest. I always kept one foot firmly planted in the secular while exploring those creeds, cults, 'isms and techniques that appealed to me – a baby-booming seeker, but no fey flower child.

So it was not the New Age with its freewheeling spirituality that drew me to Byron Bay. Nor was it the place's reputation for being one of the last bastions of individualism and a haven for alternative lifestylers (which are not always the same thing). The prospect of belonging to a small, close-knit community held some appeal and I was cheered by Thoreau's experience that 'the deeper you penetrate into the woods, the more intelligent, and, in one sense, less countrified do you find the inhabitants'. But going rural remained a gamble, for I had grown up in a small country town and still carried acute memories of the claustrophobia of one degree of separation, and of a bone-aching loneliness and ennui. Although I had holidayed in Byron and had found the natives friendly, had discovered that if you stood still for long enough in Jonson

Street, someone would offer to massage you or ask you to sign a 'Save-The-Something-Or-Other' petition, I didn't know a soul in the shire and there was no guarantee I would find my tribe.

Something else compelled me, a mighty allure that sat apart from the Rainbow Region's polyglotism and my personal considerations, and transcended them all ... It was the land – lavish, sensual, silent, benign, immutable, self-sufficient – that drew me. With its voluptuous green hills lying so close to its long white arms of beach, its hinterland waterfalls, ancient rainforests, its fecund soil, it was a pantheon of delights, its spirit as palpable as raindrops, as pervasive and transcendent as air, as immanent as in a shrine or a leaf.

But since we never perceive place with clean-slate objectivity – preconceptions, circumstances, state of mind or the lens of memory inevitably filter our apprehension – I had to acknowledge that its verdant topography reminded me in no small way of the countryside, further north, in which I had grown up.

Proust said somewhere, and amid the million and a quarter words of his magnum opus, *Remembrance of Things Past*, I can't find where, that 'the real voyage of discovery consists not in seeking new landscapes but in having new eyes'. On a metaphoric level, this claim sits verily with me. But from 1907, Proust, in order to insulate himself against the distractions of city life as well as the effect of the trees and flowers which he loved but which induced asthma attacks, rarely emerged from a cork-lined room in his Parisian apartment. If he had had the opportunity to sit like a seismological speck in the Australian landscape, he might well have conceded the pleasure and the powerful shift in perception which that experience can generate.

The more I got to know my new locale, the more the place activated my imagination and tapped into recesses of awe and desire I had no idea were within me. It would require a considerable period of quiescence and relative solitude for me to drop into the deepening receptivity that allowed insights to flow, unbidden, from Her. And the more deeply I surrendered, the longer I waited and trusted and listened, the more revitalised I would begin to feel.

But back then, crossing over the railway line on my way to temporary accommodation ('Low Cost Luxury By The Sea', where Sandy, the receptionist with a peace sign tattooed on one upper arm and a dolphin on the other, immediately picked me for an 'ego-tourist' and assured me the swimming pool was the 'state of the ark'), I anticipated none of this. Blessed with the optimism of ignorance, all I knew was that I was going to live in a place of light infusion, in this most easterly, surf's-up ecotopia, where Australia thrusts its sub-tropical belly button into the South Pacific. As for the prospect of bad weather, I was willing to take my chances.

5

____

Encountering Nature

There were halcyon days ahead, days when I felt myself happily suspended in a bubble of peerless beauty, days when I was seduced not only by the eros and bounty of the natural world, but also by the heady and unaccustomed pleasures of randomness and insouciance of such an environment.

One summer afternoon, I took a ladder from the garden shed and climbed up to watch the sunset from the vantage of one of the thick limbs of a massive old Moreton Bay fig tree on the ridge where I then lived. Metres above me, amongst its highest branches, two female fig birds were perched, occasionally emitting a variety of soft musical calls and short, sharp yelps.

To the north, a thick, fuchsia nimbus lolloped across the undulant hills while aubergine shadows swathed their eastern flanks. In the western sky, dozens of layers of stratus clouds lined up like iridescent orange highways to heaven. Across the paddock the thick, ringed stalks of a giant bamboo clump creaked and sighed like the masts of an old ship moored in a chlorophyll sea. The neighbours' big dam shimmered, an obsidian pool in the last oblique rays, and from the cool, dark core of the rainforest remnant on their property came the plangent wailings of the elusive cat bird. At twilight's end, a brigade of fruit bats wheeled and spread, blacking the sky like a stain. On their way to battle it out for roosting spots for the night, they let rip with ear-piercing squawks and screams.

In the fading light, as the landscape was repeatedly, almost imperceptibly, reframed and retinted, I breathed in plenitude and space, color and intricacy in heady measure. With the urban refugee's sharp appetite for awe, I kept swivelling my head, afraid to miss some stunning aspect, blinking to confirm my reality, almost daring the scene to shrink or vanish. Try as I might to sit in the now, I was already regretting the encroaching evanescence. I heard my own voice muttering, as if from a distant gully: 'This is what the dress rehearsal was for! This is it!' Many birds can't hear low-pitched sounds, in particular normal human speech. But I did not know that then and, afraid I'd scare off the fig birds, hushed myself into worshipful silence.

Sunset watching became a daily ritual for me that first magical summer. Sometimes I'd sit on the property's old stone fence and face the shielded body of the land due west; other times I'd hike across the adjoining paddocks, sit on a high knoll and look eastwards to the ocean. As the pink-ribbed sky steadily dimmed, I'd fix my gaze and concentrate, determined not to miss the first striking gleam of the lighthouse, that tiny matchstick sentinel in the distance. There were skies delightful and skies dolorous, there were days of calm elation and days when loneliness stuck to me like a decal. Were the highs, the melancholy and sense of oppression in the vistas, in the slanting afternoon shadows, or in me? No matter. Through the simple witnessing of this gratuitous matinee, I began to wake up to the daily miracle of existence.

One night that season, I walked to a secluded spot further along the ridge, watched a fat, yellow moon rise over the bay and did a barefoot dance on the dewy earth, to the accompaniment of the high-pitched drone of cicadas. In love with the felicitous lie of the land, yes, and pondering what on earth we'd done to inherit such extravagance ('It is said there is no such thing as a free lunch, but the universe is pretty close,' said physicist Stephen Hawking), but still far too busy, too out-there, too often on 'broadcast' and too seldom on 'receive', to develop the ears with which to hear any messages from Her.

Many moons later, while writing this book actually, I re-read an interview with another physicist, Paul Davies, in which he explained one of Einstein's deductions about light, and it struck me how much it had applied to my behaviour in those days. Davies said: 'If you have a little pulse of light receding from you and you rush after it, you will never gain on it, however fast you go. And the corollary of this is you can never run faster than light.' Neither, I might add, can you detour ad infinitum around the shadows. But the full light of that recognition came much later.

In the interim, the sun came up, the sun went down, and time brought with it some rough weather, too. Inevitably. Little would be learned in a life of sunny days, would it? Yet the vehement storms which can obliterate our old senses of identity and deconstruct our former worldviews, may also bring us the gift of a tabula rasa on which to start again. The tempests can revivify our existence, even as they wreak havoc and cause loss. The lightning bolts can fracture our eggshell egos and crack open our frangible hearts, soften them towards tender mercies – for ourselves and others. Creative droughts can force us to find new ways of expressing in the world. The oppressive, still periods can slow us down long enough for us to find out who we are apart from what we do.

Moonless nights and rainy days are ideal times to hang out in the haunted caverns of personal reassessment, to peel back the persona and taste the pith, to lose the plot and find a few clues. Lucid tears can water the garden of understanding. No one can escape, indefinitely, the evolving laws of nature. As surely as the sun will rise tomorrow, certain atmospheric patterns are forecast to appear and reappear, in new formations, in unexpected moments in the long-range weathering of our lives – and it's up to us how we choose to read and respond to them.

____

6

Developing Ears

But I do not wish to sidetrack too long. The main purpose is to build a bridge across to Her stories. Suffice it to say that in the middle of my life's journey, I, like countless others before me, 'came to myself within a dark wood whose straight way was lost'.

When I admitted this to myself, when I finally stopped spinning like a weather vane in a gale force wind, when I unravelled the tight skein of my busyness, when I let go of those habits and things I'd come to depend on for security, status, identity; when I took shelter and retreated, I began to freefall, in slow-slow-motion, into the interregnums that enabled me to begin to hear Her.

At first all I felt were nascent stirrings, flimsy and faint as butterfly wings fluttering against a dozing cheek. Then I began to receive hints, inklings in barely audible whispers, in evocative silences. Small snatches – a line or a phrase – would hang in the air like dust motes made visible by sunlight.

Anxious and impatient to produce *something* out of the lengthening lacuna into which I seemed to have sunk, my mind urgently tried to weave this growing, yet amorphous material into the background of a preconceived narrative which, it soon became apparent, did not ring true. Each day the blank paper loomed before me – large, unrelieved by a single slash of color, devoid of all but its radiant, heartless confrontation, its challenging call to creation. In vain, I struggled to find a form and a voice which would convey the questions in my head and the answers in my heart. But the way ahead was blurred by tissues of illusion. The timing was not ripe. Many experiences were still seeds in the pod, many lessons green fruit on the vine. Finally I gave up, temporarily, and put the manuscript in the bottom drawer.

Some considerable time later, after what I considered a solid period of Rest and Reassessment, I began once more to 'glance from heaven to earth, from earth to heaven' and to note the 'forms of things unknown', hoping that very soon I would be able to give these airy nothings '[a] local habitation and a name'.

Another winter (or what passes for it in the sub-tropics) arrived – the perfect time to write. From the bottom drawer I dragged out the first few draft chapters, the dozens of pages of notes, all neatly typed and categorised alphabetically and topically. Tentatively, I made a second attempt at the manuscript. But I was fatigued and the writing felt forced. Within a few days I'd developed acute bursitis and had to desist and lay up. In spring I tried a third time – and accidentally put the kitchen knife through my hand. More R & R ensued. In summer, fingers metaphorically crossed, I started typing again. Wilfully. Within a week I'd badly sprained my ankle.

Okay, I said to the Feminine Face of Fate, I can take a hint or three. It's clear I'm being held up and I need to develop patience. But what else do I need to learn, understand, experience? Surely not more rest? It seems the longer I rest, the more deeply tired I discover myself to be. I don't like it. I'm afraid that if I become any more laidback, I'll be pushing up daisies. Maybe I'm not meant to be a writer, after all. I'm sticking to gentle gardening and afternoon naps until further notice. Last time I put myself in my own hands, I ended up with a knife through one of them. So now I put myself in your hands. I surrender. Do you read me? Repeat: do you read me?

Not long after, wishing to flick the harassing ('you-should-be-doing-more-better-faster') gadflies from my mind, I went one afternoon to spend time at The Cape. I hoped to enjoy the airy elements, but also there was an enigmatic 'something' I wanted to perceive, to unfurl, to imbibe, and I had a hunch I might find it there.

As indeed I did, for on that pivotal day, the land and sea, the birds, dolphins and dazzling light conspired to peel the scales from my eyes and I was moved to realise that Nature, in Her timeless, unbounded wisdom, was a profound life tutor. That was the day I began to recognise that She was not merely an exotic backdrop for a small, modern story of my devising. She was the story. A perpetual tale of infinite magnitude, layers, permutations, possibilities.

In my previously attempted fiction, Nature, in metaphors and similes, in descriptions and plotpoints and characters' motivations, had cast Herself extravagantly, commandingly, repeatedly, shamelessly in a series of cameo roles. Like a gorgeous, mesmerising actress, She had been in danger of stealing the whole literary show. Which, after clarity finally prevailed down at the Cape, is exactly what She did do.

For I saw that Nature, Herself, was a wisewoman storyteller playing out a series of much bigger, much older scenarios for me to experience, interpret and learn from. These stories – about some of the great cycles, passages and processes of life and creation – She 'dictated' to me, for She does not have words or hands with which to write. She materialised these three-dimensional belle-lettres unexpectedly, spontaneously, sometimes subtly, sometimes magnificently through the cycling of the seasons. And I noted them down slowly and patiently, for the curve of my learning and deciphering was steep, faltering and unpredictable. Cracking even a few fragments of the mysterious, complex code of creation was, to me, as daunting as a gregarious caterpillar attempting brain surgery, but a person has to start somewhere. And so, scratching tentative vermiculations on the forbidding, blank paper, I began to transcribe what the poet Pablo Neruda called the 'pure wisdom/ of someone who knows nothing'.

My general intention, if not my precise writing gameplan, became clear, and although my pace was still languid, the green light of my heart at last was switched on in response to the new, 'truer' material. Perhaps if I remained mindful and worked in moderation, there would be no more incapacitating ailments and 'accidents'. But then again, perhaps not. The Judaeo-Christian belief that if one proceeds dedicatedly on one's spiritual path, one will be rewarded and/or protected from vicissitudes, runs deep in our western culture. And the New Age dictum that if one is diligently thinking only positive thoughts and 'living in the light', one should not encounter any illness, injury or even opposition, also has assumed plenty of weight, despite its spiritual naivety and judgmentalism and despite the overwhelming daily evidence to the contrary. For example, when I strolled down Jonson Street with my arm in a sling after the hand stabbing, I ran the gamut of unsolicited 'insights' from acquaintances, counter attendants and even an effusive backpacker into why I had 'created' this injury, what personal 'issues' it signified and a potpourri of psychobabble on how to 'deal with my stuff'. Such is life in a small New Agey enclave.

But back to the letters … They turned out to be as random and diverse as Nature Herself, but since She is never at an end, and is inexhaustibly rebirthing, transforming and producing everything in mind-boggling multiplicity, they have no 'sharp vertical peaking', no peroration.

Like Nature, they do not form a neat, logically ordered set. For I did not begin with a doctrine I wanted to prove or a barrow I wanted to push, but with questions I wanted to ask, with ideas I wanted to explore and with experiences I needed (but didn't always want) to have.

Although I had no preconceived recipe, I had a raw appetite for a rich concoction in which Nature was the key ingredient. So as the seasons passed, I trusted the scents of my prevailing passions and playfully followed various vapour trails, some redolent with possibility, others the mere whiff of a word, a one-liner or a one-second sensation which might or might not mean something, lead somewhere. I was surprised to find my own intuition and understandings mixing with science and gardening, with shallow environmentalism and deep ecology, with anthropology, mythology and cosmology, with art, music and poetry, occasionally in a lumpy consistency, but mostly in a very smooth blend.

Nature, as She continues to inform my life, my leanings and learnings, may prove to be my most enduring and inspiring teacher. She is a beautiful being, the great mother of our Earth's blood. That is why we call Her Mother Nature.

I was humbled and privileged to be Her secretary, taking down these love letters and rubrics, sometimes exultantly, sometimes painfully (even rhapsodies have their diminuendos, love letters their agonies), always gratefully.

Once I'd started this work, I realised I'd opened an exponentially expanding can of worms. Questions branched into more questions, like never-ending fractals. Some of them I am still posing, others are scattered fragments I am still *com*posing. But they are not corrosive or urgent and life may yet be long.

The following letters marked a turning point in my life and I hope they may encourage you (if you are so disposed) to develop your own personal relationship with Nature, to allow Her to resonate back to you the mother-of-wisdom voice which resides in us all. I pass them on, with love and light to you, Her Children, no matter what your age, no matter where you live on this glorious garden planet.

7

A Wing and a Prayer

The Promethean atmosphere at the Cape hit me immediately in gusty up-draughts from all directions. Three hang gliders plunged and dipped their vivid wings – yellow and shocking pink, indigo and white, green and vermilion – in such close proximity, it was amazing they didn't collide.

Up in the protected northeast crook of the headland, the ice cream man was doing such a roaring trade that he surely didn't have the time to focus on more than filling orders quickly and giving correct change to customers. I doubted that he was aware of the charming din taking place just behind his colorful van. The shrill chatter of white-cheeked honeyeaters (each no larger than my hand) in a coast banksia almost drowned out the tinkling 'Greensleeves' notes, that summer signature song of Australian ice cream vendors. I bought an ice cream and walked right up to the banksia tree that was tremulous with the tender jumpings and high-pitched vibrations of the birds. They, too, were in their own sealed universe, oblivious to outsiders like me and the distant delights which my pagan eye looked for. And found. The surf was up at Wategos Beach, the lustrous swell bobbed with black specks, a mixture of frolicking dolphins and watchful surfers in wetsuits, all of whom no doubt were swimming in their own respective realities. As naturalist Loren Eiseley wrote: 'Our identity is a dream. We are process, not reality, for reality is an illusion of the daylight – the light of our particular day.'

Trekking up the steepest incline of the hill, I took in the contoured mantle of shiny green foliage and shrubbery on the southwest, slanted and windblown by ages of sou'westers. Far below lay the vast empty sweep of Tallow Beach, the frothy white crests forever rolling in, the salt spray rising in a cloud so dense today that I knew it would be visible from the ridge several kilometres away.

By the time I'd reached the lighthouse, I'd counted fifty-three interstate number plates. I tried not to regard them as an infestation, for although I might be a local resident, I wanted to be one who is grateful for her locale rather than smug about it. I reminded myself of Thoreau's dictum that an individual might own land, but not the landscape.

Up near the lighthouse, I leaned on the crisp white guard rail and let the Cape's three-hundred-and-sixty-degree scope open up my field of vision. The tower itself was immaculate, a glaring megalith of light surrounded by the unbroken azure of ocean and sky. Tucked into the curve of the Cape were the jumbled rooftops of the Wategos Beach houses. To the west lay the emerald hinterland, to the north the grab-bag architecture of the small but growing town and the white crescent of its main beach. In the distance, the sharp peak of Mt Warning distinguished itself among the bosomy blue Border ranges. I walked across to the precipitous eastern railing and, looking down at the flinty, upright rocks implacably confronting the endless onslaught of the roiling waters,

I recalled some elementary geology of the Cape.

When the ancient super-continent of Gondwanaland started shifting, the section that became Australia had a lot of volcanic activity on the east coast, from Cape York to Tasmania. The predominant volcano on the North Coast was Mount Warning. What's left of it today is the plug of that massive old caldera. It's the largest shield volcano in the world. It stopped erupting only sixteen million years ago and the lava that oozed out of it covered the whole of the North Coast of New South Wales, except for a couple of rare areas of high land – the Cape, the remnants of Julian Rocks (the sea-bound rocky outcrops to the north) and Broken Head. These pieces of land have been virtually untouched for four hundred million years! Which partly explains why I always feel I'm in a seat of power or a cathedral when I stand on them.

I was experiencing a little vulcanism of my own. In a very short space of time, I had undertaken several big work projects and, under the intense pressure of trying to meet the various deadlines, my arms had become crippled with repetitive strain injury. This was not my first experience of the disorder – it had cropped up in varying degrees of intensity for several years, always at times of personal overextension – but this was by far the most cruel and calamitous bout. Substantially disabled, I had slipped down the greasy, twirling pole of function and was reduced to a relatively helpless state for which rest was the paramount remedy. Any keyboarding, hard copy editing or serial telephoning were out of the question. As were pegging my washing on the line, turning a doorknob, opening a jam jar or cutting up the food on my plate. The mountains of my resistance to this reduction of pace and action were turning on their fiery fulcrums. My heart was melting in a white-hot magma. It was clear that some painful, primary incandescent core was beginning to work its way to the surface.

A mantra ray drifted just below the surface of the aquamarine waters and a school of sharks circled in the foaming wash. But my attention was drawn to the heights as the shadow of a large, solitary, bird passed overhead. It wheeled slowly enough for me to make out its white head, neck and breast; the remainder of its upper parts, belly and underflight feathers were a pinkish cinnamon, tipped with black.

'Wow!' came out of my mouth. It was a brahminy kite and it seemed at once liberated, heroic and powerful. The sight of it invigorated me and made me joyous. Tracing the long arcing flight path of the kite, I felt that ancient homo sapiens envy of a bird's freedom, beauty and fluent grace. Zesty blasts of air swept around me and I cinched my jacket, buffeting myself against the wind. I looked at the kite and wished I could soar to its dizzying heights, surer even than the hang gliders of how to steer through the hidden and unpredictable cross currents that coursed through my life. And yet, I thought, I *am* that kite. That kite is me.

Mesmerised by the bird's hovering stillness, I blinked into the dazzling light, offering up to its wide, rufous wings my wordless praise of its life and maker. Suddenly it plummeted and perched on the tip of a craggy outcrop halfway down between me and the sea. It sat as fixed and proud as a totem, its rich chestnut wings tucked in close, its far-sighted eyes surveying the watery depths, its white head regal in repose. For a long time, I tuned into its stasis and the limitless power surrounding that ancient rock, asking and trusting that whatever I needed to learn at this time would be made clear to me.

My Dear Child,

I am not surprised that you felt called to seek guidance in this special place, for there is a strong magnetism about it. A vast energy field envelopes and permeates The Cape. If you sit here quietly for long enough and allow yourself to be touched by it, you can feel an extraordinary power. It is through the intention to connect, the seeking, that the finding comes.

Without the trying, the longing, you could visit The Cape many times and never even sense it is the site of an immense deva. Deva is a Sanskrit word meaning shining one or body of light. A deva is a divine being, a life force grounded in the natural world. Devas have their own highly developed intelligence, but no particular form. They are as unfettered and insubstantial as the wind moving around you. Powerful devic energy is often found near mountains and cliffs, in the vast untainted regions of the sea, in the bellies of great canyons and around certain lakes, waterfalls and rivers. These areas attract people not only because of their beauty and majesty, but also because of the power, purity, wisdom and healing qualities of their devic energies.

The devas perceive a different reality to humans. To them, all of life is comprised of these flowing energies or forces and they work delightfully and tirelessly as the 'architects' who bring into form the vegetables, minerals, animals and humans that make up life on earth. They are another stream of consciousness wishing to awaken humans to the possibility of conscious co-creation and cohabitation on Earth. If you were to ask a local resident what the symbol for Byron Bay is, they would almost certainly say the lighthouse. The deva of the Cape carries an energy of transition, and movement, of illumination and change. As a local resident, you've probably noticed that radical upheavals and readjustments seem to be part and parcel of life here.

You, too, have a hidden energy body. Indeed, this problem with your arms has developed so that you might become aware of this energy body, because you no longer want to perceive yourself as a flat physical being. You know that you have about you an electricity and a vitality that is larger than your physical being, but which has not yet been expressed. I ask you to become aware of these subtle energies – in yourself and in the natural world – not to be distracted by phenomena, but simply to acknowledge these invisible realms which make up a reality far greater than the limited physical one you know through your senses. Try not to fear these realms, but rather open yourself to trust and work with them, for they offer a wisdom which can assist in uplifting you.

The hurt in your arms is a barometer of referred pain – physical and emotional – for where you are now. Allow yourself to feel the discomfort of that box that your identity is in, the feeling that your identity is smaller than your energy being. You are wondering why you haven't expressed your full true self in this lifetime, wondering when this will happen. But understand that this is the pain you can heal now, the regret that in some ways you have not been all that you thought you could be. But regret is just a state. I encourage you not to be attached to it, for then you may think that that is all there is.

Understand that you, like every human being, are more, much more than the sum total of your physical body and actions. If you will surrender to your need for rest and healing, taking whatever time it requires, you can begin to slough off, like a snake shedding its skin, some of the concrete selves, the identities you have built up since childhood. If you will cooperate, you can use this time to restore the true balance and harmony of your own nature. Be grateful for this learning phase, for it signifies that the work of change is taking place in your ongoing evolution.

You are indeed like that kite – independent and high-flying in your own way. But to stay in balance, sometimes you need to temper that tensile self-suffi-ciency with the ability to yield. Watch the kite and you will see how effortlessly she takes advantage of the unseen eddies, circling and soaring through their secret patterns. Instinctively she knows when to flap her wings and when to glide. She knows when to be a still, benevolent witness and how to detect the portents of her own essential nourishment.

There is an opportunity for learning here. Learning could be defined simply as a change in behaviour through experience. You need to learn when to persist and when to desist, when to yield to pain in the body, to trust the messages that physical discomfort brings. But I see you have not been doing that. You have often been acting like a sleepwalker, moving somnolently ahead, arms outstretched, agitatedly, resentfully pacing the same tired, old income-producing territory or blindly looking for new horizons instead of pausing, resting long enough to wake up to a new angle of vision.

Like wings, arms can offer, extend, encircle, enclose, protect, but they can also open, acquiesce and receive. Developing true *receptivity* is a hallmark of entering the deep feminine, a healthy supple state which enables you to apprehend quickly and to receive, favourably, new ideas, suggestions, assistance, ways of being. It is not to be confused with *passivity*. A passive person is inert, submissive and abnormally unreactive.

You are accustomed to learning and growing through acting and *doing*, but it is equally possible to grow through *being*. You have overvalued activity, performance, function and have forgotten to give attention and value to your own beingness. Here now is a grand opportunity to 'chill out'. Why not try it and see what happens?

Each individual, by virtue of his or her beingness, is a part of the divine cosmos. You have, if you will allow yourself to feel it, an inherent kinship with all of nature. You in particular I see have a special affinity with the winged creatures. According to the ancient mysteries, birds are the psychic messengers between worlds; they have the power to take the prayers of hapless humans to the Divine. You need only attune to a bird on some heartfelt level and an answer will be given to the questions whose words you cannot even begin to formulate.

With love and light,

Mother Nature.

8

Wild Spirit

The voluntary disintegration of old habits is a phrase that is much easier to say than to do, especially if its execution involves doing very little when you're a person accustomed to doing rather a lot.

I've always been an early riser and worker, so as I learned, inchmeal, on the rack of reluctance, to slow down, to grow into a simpler rhythm of being which invited more contemplation, repose and grace, instead of turning on the computer first thing, I would go walking on the beach.

One morning it was stormy, misty and the wind-blown streamers of sand spiralled towards me like benign, but excited ectoplasm. Air, being a fluid, is seldom still. The gulls were taking full advantage of this free energy, soaring and gliding in streamlined proficiency. But the overcast sky and the soughing wind had reduced the amount of birdsong; even the Lewin's honeyeaters who, with their loud, ringing notes were usually among the most persistent singers, were uncharacteristically quiet, their olive chest feathers puffed out in downy defence against the chilly blast.

A lone pelican waddled slowly along the billowing hem of

the shallows. The powerful flying of pelicans has always fascinated me. They soar on thermal currents, sometimes at heights of three thousand metres. I approached this one as closely as I dared, concerned that it may have met the fate of so many of its kind in this region and irretrievably, fatally entangled its feet in the fishing lines that some fishermen so thoughtlessly leave behind, or, even worse, swallowed a fishing hook. As far as I could ascertain it looked in fine fettle and, as I drew near, it spread its three-metre wings and slowly ascended. What an indictment on our 'civilisation' that we half expect such injuriousness when we get this close to our creature friends and fellow citizens. It reminded me of the night I'd spotted a dark football shape lying suspiciously still on the verge of the road on which I lived. With a stone of dread in my chest, I approached it cautiously. An echidna. Dead, of course. A case of hit and run. There would be no court hearing over this death. Some of its spines were broken and blood trickled from its nose. I cried over its small body and sat stroking its soft, brown underbelly for a long time before lifting it, carefully, for its spikes were razor sharp, into the thick bush on the roadside.

In times gone by, before the wild creatures learned from bitter experience to avoid contact with the human race, there were instances of heart-expanding tameness and inter-species contact. In *The Sea Around Us*, Rachel Carson cites the 1913 visit of a party of men to the island of South Trinidad. During that visit, 'terns alighted on the heads of the men in the whaleboat and peered inquiringly into their faces. Albatrosses on Laysan ... allowed naturalists to walk among their colonies and responded with a grave bow to similar polite greetings from the visitors.' Carson also cites the experience of British ornithologist, David Lack on the Galapagos Island, a century after Darwin: '. . . the hawks allowed themselves to be touched, and the flycatchers tried to remove hair from the heads of the men for nesting material.'

This winter morn, the beach was a monochromatic portrait in littoral loneliness. As I strode along in my winter woollens, smelling the cold salty air, I recalled having read how certain Eskimo tribes during the nineteenth century clothed a newborn babe during the first days of its life – 'in caps made of arctic hare fur, underclothes of bird feathers, a hood made of a caribou fawn with the ears attached'. Citing this information, the author, scientist Barry Lopez, who'd come upon it in Franz Boas' book *The Central Eskimo* (1888) remarked how struck he was by the tremendous efforts of the mother to 'confirm the child immediately in a complex and intricate relationship with "the land", the future source of the child's spiritual, psychological, and physical well-being'. This ancient fellowship with the land, he believed, was 'an antidote to the loneliness that in our own culture we associate with individual estrangement and despair'. It struck me that the loving artistry and energy of expectant welcome which an Eskimo mother instilled in such garments surely must also touch the infant. And this warm welcome would lie like an invisible secondary layer atop the primary miracle of the birds' feathers themselves.

Feathers make up between five and fourteen per cent of a bird's weight and because smaller-bodied birds lose heat more rapidly than larger ones, they are usually better insulated. A ruby-throated hummingbird has 300 feathers for each gram of body weight (more than 900 feathers) while the tundra swan has only four per gram (totalling around 25,000 feathers).

Intermittently a lightning branch electrified the sky; the crack and rumble of thunder temporarily drowned out the wind and the pounding of the surf, then subsided. Thus the Earth blinked and burped occasionally as it breathed in and out, uttering its own unknowable prayers, extending to all the unending, unquestioned privilege of a place aboard. The untamed, unconditional grace of it made me draw in my own breath and release it in an indebted sigh.

My Dear Child,

Whenever you feel isolated or despondent and are trying to attune to the subtleties of the landscape, remember that the wind, your invisible brother, is as much a part of it as the sand, the birds, the trees, the rocks, the seashells. Through the treetops, he serenades you with the music of the glorious hidden spheres, for he is their beloved instrument. They wish you to know that they always embrace you and are willing and waiting to work with you if you will but remember to call on them. Keep this in mind when next you feel the whisper of the wind's tender melody on the nape of your neck or when his howling winter crescendo cuts through your thickest clothes and makes gelid your bones. For he is the most mercurial of the elements.

Although the hidden spheres (including the wind) do not wear the material raiments of your physical realm, they ask you to open your awareness to their existence. If they seem remote and separate from you, remember this is only an illusion, which occurs because in the loss of your archaic connections to nature, you have forgotten them. Truly, they are as near to you as your next breath. The wind's own breath leaves its impression in the swaying of branches, the rustling of tall grass or the billowing of sails on the sea, just as you leave a frosty imprint of your own warm exhalation on cool glass.

For the wind, every moment is an adventure as he carves clandestine trails of exploration through new territory, ascending and diving to gain fresh perspectives. Tune in to the wind when you are weary or melancholy, for he can lift up your spirits. The wind can blow the cobwebs from your mind or make you rub your eyes to create a clearer view of what is around you. He can transport you from the mire of your daily chores and cares to an expansive, light dimension beyond the highest clouds or deepest caverns.

Whirling and whistling around the planet, the wind is a constant reminder of your own wondrous breath – one of the Divine's most bountiful gifts to you. This gift is with you from the moment you are born until the moment you 'utter your last breath'. Every minute of every day you breathe in, and out, and rest. And in. And out. And rest. And so on. Automatically. Yet most of the time you take this miraculous, unceasing cycle for granted, for you are so cut off from your own creaturehood and so unaware of vital parts of yourself, that you do not know who it is who breathes within you.

Your ancient civilisations in Egypt and Greece understood the breath as the vessel of vitality, linking human beings with the Divine. The breath has always been a connecting energy that helps you to synthesise what is happening in your outer and inner realities. In its inexorable motion, it is a virtuoso musician playing the harp of your body, the rising and falling notes of your life force. It is the medium in which your voice – in speech or song – exists and travels.

Yet, amid the infinite distractions of your pacy, complex world, you have almost lost sight of this knowledge, and so your breath mostly becomes stuck in a tight, narrow groove of the same, old recording. When you forget your breath for so long, you contract, and the expansiveness of its living repertoire is not played out.

In your common speech are many refrains celebrating the significance of your breath. When you need a short pause or rest in your activities, you may take a breather. If you transgress the conventions of your society, you may become tainted with the breath of scandal. A lover may speak to you in a breathy whisper. When you've been exerting yourself, you may feel breathless and need a few moments to catch your breath. Either a beautiful sunset or a few cruel words from a loved one can take your breath away. In annoyance or frustration, you may mutter under your breath. Or ask a demanding person to leave you alone and give you a chance to breathe. When someone refuses to hear your point of view, you may recognise the wisdom of saving your breath. Young people often feel their parents are breathing down their necks. In the theatre, the director sometimes needs to breathe confidence and gusto into the actors, to strengthen and elevate their performances. When the police want to test to see if you are driving under the influence of alcohol, they breathalyse you.

See how ever-present and pervasive that maestro, the breath, is?

You expend so much energy striving to achieve, to improve, to make your life 'work' and to 'get it right,' according to your plan, that most days you leave very little space to simply be. Some days it is enough to rise and remember to breathe the gifted air, the oxygen you take in courtesy of the green plants. This exchange of breath – you breathing out carbon dioxide which the plants then inhale, and their breathing out oxygen for you to inhale – is part of the constant, often unconscious communion of life you share with the Earth. Fuelling this life-sustaining exchange of energy is the sunlight which, like your daily breath, you mostly take for granted.

I encourage you to take even as little as five minutes each day, to sit quietly, close your eyes and gently focus on your breath. This practice will begin to link you to a deep appreciation of how your every heartbeat and every breath have been given to you by the plants through the food chain. Over time, this practice also will help you to find your own true life rhythm, to sense when to act and when to rest, when to advance and when to recede, when to speak and when to remain silent.

What's more, when you sit and connect with that part of you that breathes – the breather within, if you like – you start to experience that you are more multi-dimensional than you generally allow yourself to recognise.

Conscious breathing purifies your physical body, helps you to stay in the moment, connects you to your deeper, imperishable self and allows you to open your energy body. You don't always need to understand or interpret that energy with your mind. Just breathe normally and let yourself feel. Let your thoughts and feelings be waves of energy passing through your body as easily as the wind weaves through the trees. Don't try to hold that energy. Let it move and release by breathing in and out, in your own personal rhythm.

And for goodness' sake, my child, don't hold your breath. You keep thinking that if you hold your breath, set your jaw and soldier on, you won't feel your wounds – the griefs and losses, the fears and furies that inevitably are experienced in life. But understand that if you hold your breath for too long, you're going to die.

Even wine tastes better after you allow it to breathe a while. So give yourself the same opportunity. Tilt your face towards the wind. Trust in his benevolence, as you trust in your own conscious breath to help you to relax, to smell the roses or the eucalypts, the refinement or the richness in each moment.

With love and light,
Mother Nature.

9

Wanganui

On the way to Wanganui Gorge on a mid-summer's day, it was hard not to think about trees, its main attraction. Tall congregations of them cloaked the shoulders of the winding dirt road in, sheltering the wayfarer from the scorching sun, whispering soft hosannas through the hint of breeze.

Back in the 1840s, when the settlers and cedar cutters arrived in these parts, there were many, many more trees, of course. The whole region was known as The Big Scrub, which then was the largest continuous tract of sub-tropical rainforest in Australia and was estimated to have exceeded 75,000 hectares. Of that original area, only about 100 hectares or 0.13 per cent now remains as small, isolated remnants.

It was during that extended phase of clearing when 'the work of nature over thousands of years was ... undone by the selector's axe' that a local, a Mr D. McIntyre, penned the words of the *Song of the Big Scrub*. These lines typified the white man's prevailing attitude to nature:

'Where your children are devoted to the land their parents
  wrested
From the stubborn force of Nature in the pioneering days.'

By the 1980s a growing community land ethic (that the natural environment is critical to human meaning and fulfilment) had begun to develop, yet rainforest ecologist and eco-philosopher Len Webb was moved to note: 'It is a sad commentary on the state of our knowledge that metres of book shelves in conservation libraries sag with the weight of tomes devoted to the horrors of deforestation and the disappearance of the world's rainforests, yet only a few centimetres are so far occupied by books that deal with the theory and practice of reforestation in presently degraded rainforest lands. We have beaten our breasts long enough. Let us now bend our backs!'

In 1996, at least one more centimetre of shelf space was added by local resident Rob Kooyman in his book, *Growing Rainforest*. A ranger and forest assistant for more than twenty years, Rob's reforestation on his own property is a testament to his knowledge and commitment to re-greening the land. We had a long yarn about trees one day and Rob said: 'I believe that we are an inherent part of the planet, and that our separation from nature is the basis of most of our "ills".' Rob claims that restoration ecology may well be the ultimate expression of homage to nature by the biophilic. Despite minimal promotion, the steady sales of Rob's book constitute one small refreshing fact amid the arid statistics of worldwide deforestation. Biophilia, it appears, may be more prevalent than is currently documented. Although Rob claims that trees are sentient and social, preferring to live in groups as much as humans do, he says he's not interested in growing trees per se. 'I'm interested in the ecological interaction between trees and the wildlife. In reforestation, wildlife is the barometer of your success. They know when you've got it right.'

Trees, according to religious scholar and author Matthew Fox, 'were the first creatures to stand up. That's one reason we have a special affinity to them ... when we overcome being couch potatoes and stand up.' I parked the car, stood up and walked down into the belly of Wanganui. The walking trail, which originally was carved through the woods as a bullock track, took me across a narrow, rickety wooden bridge and through red carrabeen, guioa, cudgerie, brush box, water gums, maiden's blush, red cedar, black apple, crab apple, tree ferns and white beech, through yellow carrabeen and blue quandong with their huge flying buttresses, and on towards that show-stopper of the rainforest – a gigantic strangler fig. The fig looked antediluvian, brazenly wearing its aerial roots and arteries, its strangling sinews on its trunk, just like Superman wears his underpants on the outside. A giant pepper vine, part of it as thick as my neck, also looped its way around the massive buttress root and trunk. As Sandy, the tattooed motel receptionist might have remarked: they were all hanging on by the skin of their sheath.

To reach the fig, I had to negotiate piles of mossy black boulders hurled up and artfully strewn by nature who knows how many millennia ago. Crows nests, delicate ferns and even saplings sprouted from these sheer rocks. The place was moist, pulsing with its own fertile force, so alive and yet so private, it was impossible not to feel an intruder. Mindfully, I stepped across fallen, rotting tree trunks chocolate with age and maculated with mosses and delicate, finger-length ferns. When I reached the fig's deep buttress, I took a deep breath and leaned my body into it. By some fortuitous quirk of fate or divine intervention (same thing really) this vestal remnant pocket, this temenos of trees, had escaped the clear felling which erased most of the Big Scrub and, as I stood in the fig's knotty embrace, I found myself respectfully and gratefully inclining my brow to that grace.

Donald Culross Peattie, known for his insightful nature writing, explained pragmatically and poetically that chlorophyll, 'is the one link between the sun and life; it is the conduit of perpetual energy to our own frail organisms. From inert and inorganic elements – water, and carbon dioxide of the air, the same air that we breathe out as waste – chlorophyll can synthesize with the energy of sunlight. Every day, every hour of all the ages, as each continent, and equally important, each ocean, rolls into the sunlight, chlorophyll ceaselessly creates. Only when man has done as much, may he call himself the equal of a weed. Plant life sustains the living world – more precisely, chlorophyll does so. Blood, bone and sinew, all flesh is grass. The wealth and diversity of our material life is accumulated from the primal fact of chlorophyll's activity. The roof of my house, the snapping logs upon the hearth, the desk where I write, are my imports from the plant kingdom. For fundamentally, and away back, coal and oil, gasoline and illuminating gas had green origins too.

'We, then, the animals consume those stores in our restless living. Serenely the plants amass them. They turn light's active energy into food, which is potential energy stores for their own benefit. Animal life lives always in the red, obeying the thermodynamic law that energy runs forever downhill. It is the stuff of life that rebels at death. Only chlorophyll fights up against this current. It is the mere cobweb on which we are all suspended over the abyss.'

On the track back, I pulled up short when, a few metres ahead, a primeval-looking lace monitor emerged from the thick scrub and foraged on the sunlit ground before slinking into the vegetation on the other side.

Back on the causeway, I stood delighting in the chill of Cooper's Creek running over my bare feet. The place smelled fresh and pungent after recent rain. To the west stood the imposing rhyolite cliff face, a tall, stark backdrop, branded by the sun at its apogee, yet seemingly impervious to the tempests of aeons. Upstream a large, black boulder in the shaded verge beckoned me. I clambered across a clumpy margin of muddy grasses and a host of odd-sized stepping stones to reach it. Sitting on its cool, smooth back, I let some of my cumulative tiredness flow out through the soles of my submerged feet and away with the water. A hiss of insects injected the steamy air, and above this, a crimson rosella, high in a water gum, sang a mellow descant with its piping whistle.

Like a pilgrim, I sat and listened and looked, engorging the pleasing particularities, the inviolable forces of the place. The firmness of the rocks, the resistance of the cliffs, the rasping of the creek, the untrammelled trees all spoke to me of their riches – their solidarity, their integrity, their uncontaminated air of existence. My toes twitched in response to a tickle, a broad brown leaf floating downstream.

I felt further layers of lassitude fall away from me. Yet underneath those surface layers were several more strata of it – older, thicker, petrified by decades of driven doing and obeisance to those inner voices urging me to: 'Achieve more!' and 'Measure up!' My reptilian brain was programmed to depend upon will and reasoning, heroic industriousness and productivity for economic survival. But my spirit was calling out for me to lie down in other green pastures, to reclaim faith and feeling as my primary guiding motivations. And my body (the body being a receiving station for signals from the soul) was flashing the amber lights of its ailing, trying to wake me up to this need by becoming an ergonomic refusenik.

Those ingrained, weary layers oppressed me till it was too much of an effort to sit upright on that rock. So I high-stepped my way across the boulders and stones to the stream's bank, and there, amongst the cool comfort of the tall trees, I spread my jacket on the leafy debris and lay down to be revived by a vital force beyond my singular power.

In being with nature I was beginning to learn that what you see is often mere froth atop the deep waters of what you get.

My Dear Child,

I am pleased that you have come to visit me in this great gorge. To create it, I played with a vast emerald palette, applying its many tints to form the rich textures and lavish layers among which you may now – if you will relax – feel yourself immersed and welcomed.

For you are not separate from my tableau verdant, but a welcome and integral part of its ever-changing variety and splendour. Indeed, your being here is as glorious and sacrosanct as anything you see about you.

Breathe in deeply now. Allow your shoulders and your buttocks to sink down and feel the support of the earth.

There is nothing to do and nowhere else to be, but here.

I see that your vitality is depleted. Do not be despondent about this. Be patient. Understand that if you have sprinted forty frantic paces into a dark forest and collapsed there, it will take time and rest and more than forty slow-walking paces to emerge from it. You have created this phase as an opportunity, an excuse if you like, for rest, self-examination and reorienting, all of which you need, but somehow do not feel entitled to.

So try to relax into it and trust that it, like all life cycles, it will eventually complete itself. Physical healing takes time and spiritual healing may sometimes take even longer – and cannot be speeded up. It brings its own opportunities. You would not be able to plumb the depths and mysteries in a lifetime jammed on fast-forward, would you?

Allow yourself to enjoy this repose, to absorb my green gift of renewal, as naturally as you breathe in and out in your own rhythm.

Know that nature has much to give you now. The trees, the flowers, the birds, the rocks, the earth, the stream ... These are all benevolent thought made solid; they are love, unconditional love, made manifest. Love is just a vibration that you extend to others – your parents, your siblings, your children, your lovers, your friends. And if they do not always love you back as you love them, that is alright. The love you send out will always return to you from somewhere else in the cosmos. Do not judge where that love comes from, beloved, for it is all ultimately from the same source. It is all the same giving, the same transmission, the same healing, the same learning, the same vibration, the same flow. The same love.

Like that leaf which did wash over your feet, allow yourself to float easily now along the surface stream of your own thoughts.

It is time to be still, to effortlessly merge with the natural elements, for you are an inseparable part of the living stream of all life. Allow yourself to offer up to the stream your most private thoughts and dreams, your secrets and memories, your pains and past conditioning, for they are part of the priceless treasury that comprises your life, this lifetime.

In return, the stream will carry you through a reverie and down into the fluid, wordless arcana of its long lifetime, in to the silence of your heart's inner chambers.

And as it takes you on this journey, allow the busyness of your mind to drop away as a stream will drop over a final precipice, and into a placid deep pool below.

When you permit yourself to drift in this effortless void of being, time melts like honey on the tongue of the water, linking you to the healing heart of the Earth, to the collective wisdom and compassion of its innumerable lifetimes.

In your memory, set aside a special space in which to store today's serene, stretchy moments, for each one is a talisman of truth to be carried forward and retrieved when you may need it.

And although you cannot always come here, you

can take some time each day, no matter where you are, to withdraw from the distractions and demands of the outer world and be still in the eternal garden of the spirit.

With love and light,
Mother Nature.

10

The Grand Design

When a cool whiff of breeze rent my repose, I realised that at least two hours must have passed. The sun had moved on and now the height and density of the trees oppressed me. The gorge had become chthonic, a chaotic green underworld in whose centre I felt claustrophobic, diminished and afraid.

Yet the ominous shadow of impermanence loomed even more menacing than the shade cast by the tallest trees. The ravine, in all its rampant, tendrillous lushness, became a poignant spectre of loss to me.

I retraced my steps to the causeway and up the slight dusty incline to the car. On the drive home, my view of the landscape described mad, pendulous swings, from sensual appreciation to fear of survival. The miles-long cathedrals of trees on Wilson's Creek Road, how long would we have them? Cruising along Coolamon Scenic Drive, I drank in the pleasing symmetry of the land, the sinuous, green ridge rising sharply from the narrow tract of coastal plain, the sweeps of alabaster beach fringed by the sapphire sea.

From the high dirt road of St Helena, this vista of the lowlands already bore the gashes and scars of quarries, of roads and encroaching housing. Can we ever truly fathom the eternal mystery of the land? Perception and personal disposition always overlay, occlude. On an optimistic day, I could look at that plain lying verdantly clothed, or I could see it as I did this day, spread in naked jeopardy, a vulnerable, irresistible object of conquest for the rapacious forces of greed and pernicious destruction, those heavy corporate dudes who, in the slick guises of progress and growth, get their jollies by cutting a merciless swathe through the virgin countryside.

By then I was only a few minutes' drive from my cabin, but I could hardly look at a stand of trees without fearing for their loss. The hills and paddocks strafed for dairying depressed me. What to do? What to do? What could an individual do? And what difference would it make? I repaired and recycled and never let the tap run when I brushed my teeth, but every time I drove my car, turned on a light switch or put my garbage into a plastic bag which would survive in a landfill for a thousand years, I knew I was not doing the planet any favours. Aware of these non-negotiable truths, I'd get myself so corseted with guilt, I'd think: Well excuse me for breathing.

My own excursions into political activism had constituted one segment of a centrifugal, production-oriented way of living which had led to a chronic dissipation of energy and a blind visionary vortex. SUBVERT THE DOMINANT PARADIGM! said the green bumper sticker, but the more embroiled I had become in 'the battle', the more that pessimistic, patriarchal model, with its endless loop of adversarial machinations, had tyrannised me, worn me down and flattened my spirits. For me there had to be more; there had to be a way of thinking and contributing beyond that rigid, restrictive, war-torn paradigm, and I was willing to travel to the antipodes of my cyclonic lifestyle to find it.

Joseph Campbell, who spent a lifetime exploring and explaining the mythical pathways relevant to our contemporary lives, held up a mirror for me with his observation that: 'Instead of clearing his own heart, the zealot tries to clear the world ... (with good conscience, and indeed a sense of pious service).'

Sociologist and author Peter Bishop had this insight: 'Concern about ecology seems to promote ceaseless activity. The problems are always presented as *urgent*, the question always what to *do now*! Contemplation has been replaced by activism.' And academic-author David Tacey, threw further light on matters with his contention that: 'Ecology almost looks like a pragmatic and secular activity, and devotion to the needs of the environment may not cause the same embarrassment that devotion to the spirit would generate.' Surely the two realms, the spiritual 'inside' and the physical 'outside,' were conterminal, I reasoned, although my education and upbringing had provided no formal or traditional framework for such a belief.

When I got home, I realised I had a case of what Chinese medicine calls 'too much head', so I put on my gumboots and went stamping across the hills, plunging down the gullies till it was twilight, till my hamstrings hurt, my breath was ragged and my ears rang with the pounding praise of my own red rushing existence. I sat down on a rocky outcrop, still warm from the sun's rays. As I focussed on allowing my breath to slow down, the claw of grief and guilt in my diaphragm loosened its grip. Among the ghostly limbs of a dead gum tree, a convention of ravens came to roost, one by one, their glossy plumage adumbrated against the retreating light, their nasally 'aah-aah-aah-r-r's' drifting down the gully like dying gurgles. Unaware of the possibility of planetary pulverisation, those wild black birds nevertheless sat poised for their own takeoff cues, so invisible and inexplicable to me.

So many aspects of the avian world continue to be a revelation to me – like their farsightedness even while flying at low altitudes. 'A nomadic flock of ravens flying at fifty metres can probably scan more than a kilometre on each side of the flight path.' Like humans, birds have their own territorial concerns. A pair of ravens (who mate for life) will, on average, defend an area of one hundred and ten hectares against trespass by other ravens.

All at once, they squawked and spread their generous wings, and in their unencumbered ascent, I felt my spirits lifted up. At that moment it seemed savvier to believe in those creatures than in any highfalutin' ideology, easier to make peace with them than with my own apocalyptic concerns.

My Dear Child,

I see that, like so many of my progeny, you are concerned about the Earth and questioning your place and purpose here. If you will, for a little while allow yourself to hang out, as your surfies, your hippies and similarly relaxed tribes are wont to say; if you will stop flagellating yourself long enough to listen, I have a few things to share with you.

It is true that in these times, aggressive ecological

activism has an important role to play, pitted as it is against the behemoth of your industrial economy, and some of you will find this a challenging and energising call. But the Green Movement will never fully succeed while so many of those enlisted in its cause fight the good fight under the pall of their own personal psychic shadows, wearing on their sagging shoulders the epaulettes of self-righteousness, self-redemption and expiation of personal guilt through good Green deeds. In these cases, self-interest often masquerades as selflessness.

Many environmental footsoldiers live in fear of the day when they won't have any more wars to wage, for where will they then hurl all the hand grenades of their own undetonated emotional arsenal – their stockpiled rage (however fluent and persuasive), their unattended, suppurating wounds and other miscellaneous maladies of their individual and collective psyches?

Only when sufficient numbers of those enlisted in this cause have cleared enough heavy clouds from their own inner atmospheres will the movement become sufficiently empowered, enlightened and charismatic to attract the widespread enthusiasm and devotion it needs from the general population – and ipso facto the entrenched power structures of business and government – to make a real difference to life on Earth.

And by that time its high priests and priestesses (not admirals and generals) will be operating from a very different premise of power – one that embodies compassion, that promotes your common identity with all that abides in the biosphere and beyond, one that focusses more on the beauty than on the terror of that wide brown island you live on, one through whose veins are running not the clotted poisons drawn out by locking horns with the patriarchy, but a clear flow of positive promises of the wondrous partnership (with nature) possibilities that lie ahead of us. It is chiefly through harnessing and distributing energies of this calibre on a worldwide scale – and not through the scare tactics, crying victim and guilt trips (wearing thin these days) – that substantial change will be brought about in the days to come.

Through history as you perceive it, many fine women and men have given their energies, their skills, money, contacts and support to causes. But these folk trusted their own intuitions and did not feel their purpose in life required them to be someone or something different from what they inherently were. They did not latch on to causes hoping to meld the aims of those causes with their own unrecognised ones. These people clearly saw the value and significance of their own *beingness* – and then added their own individuality and dynamism to causes to become even *more* of their essential selves. They were propelled by enthusiasm and optimism, a desire to expand personally, by a sense of exploration and by love – and not by fear!

Of course, not everyone feels called to be an ecowarrior. Among you will be those who choose to contribute in another way. For many of you, nature is the environment in which your self-knowledge and creativity is birthed and nurtured. It is the matrix (from the Latin womb) in which and through which your desire to reawaken people to their love of the planet can be expressed, ritualised and celebrated. It may be through art or sculpture, dance or music, poetry or prose, through public speech or private contemplation. There are countless ways to be of service on the Earth. And it really makes no difference what you do – retire to an Indian ashram or head up the local chapter of Greenpeace, become a gardener or a neurosurgeon, a cook or a counsellor, a parent, teacher or a tennis player. Just as I do not judge you, I ask you not to judge any one person's life path as being more appropriate or effective than another's. Each person is free to contribute in their own way to the marvellous mosaic of life. You are beginning to appreciate the value of biodiversity in the wilderness; well, biodiversity among peoples serves the same essential purpose.

What matters is your willingness to heed life's demands as they arise, to put aside wilful desire and respond to what is being asked of you from moment to moment, from year to year. It may happen that just when you are burning with evangelistic zeal to fix up the world through a breathtaking blur of worldly activity, what you most need to do is to retreat, take stock and commune alone with the Infinite. Or it may happen that just when you're longing to withdraw into meditation and solitude, your help is required in the outer world. Such are the challenging paradoxes of the spiritual life; the clarion calls to change. And ultimately, your world can only be changed if the people living in it change themselves. Attempting change only on the outside is like painting the body-work of one of those rusty, old pollution machines (cars, you call them) you all drive – while ignoring the faults and failings in the engine.

These times in which you live over-emphasise the outer world, the world of action, and underestimate both the restorative value of contemplation and the healing power of the natural world. Your participation in a spiritual relationship with me has not only been dangerously neglected, but almost completely overlooked.

Although humankind has mercilessly plundered and degraded Earth's life-giving resources, I do not condemn you. I still envision a grand future for us, one born of co-creation. You have many more lessons to learn about living in harmony with me and how could you begin to learn those if I withdrew my inexhaustible gifts of awe and inspiration? For when you harness these dynamic energies, then can much be changed and healed, individually and collectively, locally and globally. It is all part of the one great uplifting.

Never underestimate the power of divine invocation. Each time you sit in spiritual communion, asking for help for yourself or for others, remember also your Great Mother Earth, this bijou in the cosmos. Give thanks for her immeasurable profusion and abundance, her infinite diversity, her depth, her beauty and strength.

Call down onto her vast crenellated face all the light of all creation and petition the healing not only of her body, but of the bodies and minds of all those aboard her. Humbly ask for the highest good for the whole congregation of life here to be made manifest. Saturate the airwaves with your dreams and prayers for this evolution, for your good is linked inexorably with hers. She it was who birthed you and it is upon her continued health that you must depend for your sustenance, for your very survival in the physical terms with which you identify.

With love and light,
Mother Nature.

Waiting for Sunshine

People who visit this area often wistfully express a desire to live amid its verdancy, to which I'm inclined to reply: 'I hope you like rain.' It rains a lot here – on average, 74.5 inches annually, depending on whether we get a cyclone. Rain can set in, with few clear interruptions, for months. Despite its inconveniences – clothes won't dry, leather shoes and odd household items grow mould, and when it's torrenting I can't go walking abroad – I enjoy the way it cleanses the atmosphere and blunts the prismatic light.

The Earth's first rain fell more than four thousand million years before humankind arrived on the scene. 'Water is a great menstruum of ''life'',' wrote the physiologist Sir Charles Sherrington. 'It makes life possible. It was part of the plot by which our planet engendered life. Every egg-cell is mostly water, and water is its first inhabitant.'

The alchemists of the Middle Ages believed that if a fragment of the Philosopher's Stone were floated on the surface of water, the whole process of creation would occur in miniature, facilitating the complete story of the evolving of the universe to 'be perceived by the experimenter'. And the sixteenth-century physician, astrologer and prophet, Nostradamus, was said to have read the future through water-gazing. 'Sitting at night in a candle-lit loft, using various herbal mixtures and alchemical processes, he would gaze into a brass bowl, uttering ancient occult words and passing into deep trances.'

In the 1980s, after four years of experiments, a well-established French scientist, Jacques Benveniste carried out, in collaboration with twelve other scientists, studies that confirmed the ability of water to retain the 'memory' of molecules it once contained. Their experiments, published in 1988 by *Nature*, one of the most influential of all scientific journals, showed that if solutions of antibodies were diluted repeatedly until they no longer contained a single molecule of antibody, they still produced a response from immune cells. If their findings are accurate, the laws of biochemistry would need to be completely rethought, the claims of homeopaths would be validated and extremely dilute substances shown to have a possible effect on the human body. The scientific community reacted violently to Benveniste's claims about the memory of water, calling them a 'delusion'. Benveniste counter-claimed he had become the victim of a witch-hunt and of repression and censorship in the scientific community.

Whether or not water possesses a remembrance of things past may still be in dispute, but one thing is certain – H_2O remains essential to plant and animal life on Earth, and we waste, pollute or take it for granted at our peril.

One whole rainy season (after I moved to live by the beach and while I was on a self-prescribed sabbatical), I spent resting, reading, playing the piano, looking at the bare patches where more garden was yet to be made, imagining which plants I would put in, and wondering in which direction my life was heading, or rather, waiting for a sign that it was going anywhere at all. By mid-season, things got so still and quiet, sepulchrally quiet, that one day, needing some respite from the 'silence' (that dreaded chasmic, not cosmic, reality) and from the arguing voices and clamouring absurdities inside my head, I put on Vaughan Williams' *The Lark Ascending* and, taking up a fine-tipped brush, began to detail my old furniture, picture frames and curios with gold leaf. Also, I retrieved my seventy-odd flying wall birds from a packing case in which they had flown south for several winters and, with the help of A-ral-dit-e[1], the goddess of broken ceramics, began to mend those in need. Several days and tubes of acrylic and glue later, I caught my grimacing face in the cruel morning light of my bathroom mirror. My left hand gripped an old toothbrush with which I was fastidiously scraping the grouting.

Another day while pottering in the garden between heavy downpours, I noticed the short stump of a cordyline cutting I'd planted six months earlier. Despite my having watered, fertilised and mulched it during that time, it showed no signs of growth. It still looked like a dead stick jutting from the earth. An impatient fit of pique descended on me. I wanted a tall, luxuriant plant to adorn this somewhat bare corner of the garden. If I nipped down to the nursery, I could buy a mature plant. Now! And so I yanked the cordyline stem out of the dirt, only to find a small but sturdy white root sprouting from its base underground. Apart from admonishing myself for brutishly hefting about this divine, living manifestation of substance as if it were mere incidental matter, I suddenly felt imbued with a deep trust – trust that every organic creation has its own mysterious, but natural rhythm of growth, its own process of fulfilling. Evidently a lot of expanding and establishing needed to take place in the dark underground before what was above ground could begin to sprout and flourish.

What did I, a subatomic speck of stardust in the cosmological scheme of things, know about appropriate timing? What right did I have to expect nature to fit into my small, self-interested schemes and schedules?

My Dear Child,

The cosmos has a lot to teach you about the fruits that waiting and patience can bear. According to your scientists, it waited fifteen billions of your years for you to be born into this lifetime, and now that you are here, you have your own purpose to fulfil, your own destiny to live out.

However, your destiny does not always unfold as you consciously wish or imagine it to be. Throughout your life you will find yourself waiting – to make a crucial decision, to receive an answer to a question you've asked, for a shift in circumstances, for a fortuitous connection, for a talent to be recognised, a skill to be honed, for an opportunity to present itself, even for things as apparently prosaic as the passing of time or a break in the weather.

To wait is to hold yourself in readiness for something. While you wait, try to remain receptive to your inner and outer worlds, not passive. (Remember the difference I explained that day you saw the kite at the lighthouse?)

Waiting, if you will surrender to the process, can be a meditation, a rite of passage (a way of consciously travelling from one condition of life to another) in itself. Significant change can take place while you're waiting – *if* you will focus your attention on your own nature. While you wait, try to stay in the present and to surrender to the silence, for it will direct you into the depth of yourself. Spiritual surrender is most misunderstood in your times. It does not entail action. It is not a negative state and does not involve the failure, inertia, resignation, defeat or giving up that worldly surrender implies. Rather it is a way of yielding, of favourably receiving and accepting your circumstances instead of resisting them. It involves relinquishing the personal will and deferring to a framework of wisdom greater than your mental perception, and when entered into fully, it can be an exalted state, even if only momentarily. But do not set yourself up to 'succeed' at surrender or it will surely elude you. Surrender, like forgiveness, like grace, does not descend in one final curtain call; it makes its own quiet entrances into your life, in increments, over time. Its role in the story of your physical life is never over until you leave the body.

While you wait, nurture yourself as you would a tender seedling or sapling. Give yourself the time and space to grow. Fertilise the ground of your own awareness. Ask to be shown where you are blocked in your thoughts or emotions; ask for help in freeing the blockages and developing the right attitude to foster your own advancement. Allow those behaviours that do not serve you to drop away, as leaves from a tree in autumn.

The right time to move or act will present itself, so do not try to pre-empt that time. For as you have learned from your time in the garden, if you prune a plant too early, it will not blossom.

While you wait, it may appear that nothing is happening, but if you are attending to your inner nature, a lot of deep, hidden growth is actually taking place, as you did see with that young cordyline plant. This underground activity is the source from which – like a river that begins as a trickle high in the mountains – all change in your outer world flows. Indeed, the universe cannot address itself to your needs until this inner transformation is underway.

In ancient times, people cultivating the land would set aside a sabbatical year during which certain parts of the land were to be left fallow, to allow them to regain fertility for a new crop. In the same way, it may happen sometimes that your waiting involves a period of reduced worldly activity, of sitting very quietly and going within, of deep rest and recuperation. Try not to fear that place, for although it may be dark, it is like a womb in which you can begin to hear the embryonic voice of your own deeply wise counsel, that innate wisdom which dwells in every human being, waiting, sometimes for many years, or even lives, to be called upon, befriended. Let yourself drop into that still, safe place – when you are meditating or listening to music or watching the clouds drift by. Trust in the healing and growth that can occur there and know that the season of outer movement and change will recycle itself in your life, in due course.

Meanwhile, you may find yourself wavering, wondering, withdrawing, not knowing and being afraid of the future. This is just the time to *be* with your uncertainty, ambiguity, confusion; to conserve your energy, to sit, planless, mapless and accepting in the hub of uncertainty, for it is within that matrix that many possibilities are rising and falling, waiting to be realised or discarded. It is enough sometimes to mentally play with these ideas; to entertain them, to let them advance and recede, to state your intent if you have a clear one. Perhaps your intent is not yet clear. That is alright. If you wait, your intent eventually will emerge from the vast unconscious pond of being and the appropriate way forward will become clear.

If you don't heed the need to wait, if you cannot trust that the divine spark within you has a more splendid and ingenious plan for your life than you can (as yet) consciously begin to imagine; if you persist in forging ahead wilfully in the face of all indications to pause, then be prepared for trouble, upheaval, redoubled difficulties, tension, loss, or ill-health. For this is what happens when you resist what the Chinese people have long called 'cosmic order'; when you try to outwit your own self-made fate. This is a difficult idea for Westerners to grasp, I know. Let me put it this way: imagine the planetary chaos that would erupt if all of nature were to run amok the way you are sometimes driven to do – if the tides decided to flow in ahead of schedule each day; or if the fruit trees tried to yield a season earlier; if the sun insisted on rising earlier and setting later; if the birds decided to migrate a season sooner.

Remember: from the deepest level of your being, you are creating each moment of your own reality and, just as the forces of nature operate with certain physical limitations, you, too, can make responsible choices within the parameters of what is possible while waiting.

Indeed, it often happens that the less you know, the more you understand. Your world is crowded with 'experts' who factually know a great deal, but this type of knowledge is no substitute for wisdom. And wisdom often grows from the cultivation of patience and trust that life is unfolding in your best interests. Your life may not look 'harmonious' in the static or balanced sense you've come to understand that word, but ultimately even the greatest hardships, the longest delays, can serve your highest good. 'Suffering' serves no purpose as an end; its true value is as a means of nudging you to grow spiritually.

With love and light,

Mother Nature.

P.S. About that rhododendron (Rhoda, I've heard you call her) you're intending to give away to your friend Michael. Do not act hastily, for if you will only wait a little longer, you will see that she will give birth to bunches of beautiful orange blooms in her own time. There is no need to uproot her.

1. Araldite: Trademark. A strong epoxy resin best known as a glue or adhesive.

Where the Garden Takes You

Creating a garden was an absorbing experience for me, a lurid baptism in the senses – brushing against the soft claret underside of a jungle velvet leaf or the fine fronds of a tree fern, having my thoughts drowned out by rowdy morning birdsong, imbibing colors vibrant and subtle, smelling the living soil after a sun-shower, tasting a nectar-laden bloom on a honey gem grevillea and feeling the spark in my heart being kindled by the fascinating, momentary effects of the light.

Mid-spring when my friend Geoff Williams was painting a mural in a part of my garden, we spoke about the power of light. He said, 'Light is everything. It's a pleasure to paint. The contrast of light against shadow or vice versa, it's like a drug. You get addicted to it.'

What about darkness and shadow? I asked. Did it not provide the contrast, the added depth and dimension without which light could never shine?

'In art,' he explained, 'the darkness is a given and light is what you learn to impose on that.' In art teaching, he said, darkness was rarely discussed, virtually overlooked. 'We're fascinated by the extremities of dark and light, yet most of life is lived somewhere in between the two.'

As the days went by, I became an ardent plantswoman, the making of the garden became a labour of love and I began to feel a sacred alliance with nature. In response, She worked Her own transfiguring magic on me, blessing me with feelings of replenishment, creative satisfaction and a host of small gratitudes that seemed to have been stored up waiting for me to express them. And so I began to give thanks for the languid flap of a banana leaf, for the silent landings of superb fairy wrens, for the rambling spread of native violets, for the growing swathes of green, for the fertility of the dark, swampy soil, for the sun's comforting heat on my back as I toiled.

Simple actions like washing my gardening tools and my hands, loosening the loamy fragments that clung to my cuticles and under my nails, became rewarding codas to the day.

Sometimes I was cheerfully lost in the sheer, wilful slog of gardening, and sometimes, when I was more receptive to what nature had to offer me, the hairs on my arms and the back of my neck stood on end and I fell into an effortless rhythm of being, hearing and doing. 'That mulberry tree needs fertilising. The azaleas need mulching.' And so on, for hours or days at a time. Despite my meagre gardening experience, I soon found myself tuned in to a perceptual frequency which broadcast not only the garden's requirements, but also the infinite, eternally fruitful resources and grace of the universe. It was as if the devas came and danced so merrily in my own Kirlian field that I found my mind 'Annihilating all that's made/To a green thought in a green shade'.

Sometimes this diffuse awareness evolved when I was active in the garden, and sometimes I was taken even more 'out there' while lazing about on the deck, watching the bright tiara of light around it gradually recede as the hours slid by. Gazing with a rapt, satisfied emptiness at the partly completed garden beds and idly making my future plans for them, I'd see a film or body of mist in a shady section. The first few times this happened, I thought my eyes were clouding over from too much vacant staring, so I'd blink and rub my eyelids. The mist would still be there, an unexplained signal on the radar screen of my senses.

About this accompaniment, I never became blasé. I accepted it as a gift, as part of the voyage I was making into the non-human realms, into a communion with the Others, as part of my growing awareness of the inter-relatedness of everything – seen and unseen, large and small – in nature's network. My feet were firmly on the ground (and just as often *in* it), yet such experiences could be moving. I had not expected to meet mysticism, (that oceanic feeling of unity with Nature) so prosaically while digging in the dirt, but such experiences will sometimes visit us when we are least looking for them. As the Chinese philosopher, Chuang-tzu so poetically encapsulated it: 'I do not know whether I was then a man dreaming I was a butterfly, or whether I am now a butterfly dreaming I am a man.'

My Dear Child,

If you will allow yourself to completely bring your consciousness – and nothing else – into the garden, you will be able to enter another dimension of consciousness. That dimension of consciousness is known as the devic kingdom/queendom.

If you removed the covering called physical reality, you would see human beings are in essence pure light. You all emit a glow that is made up of many, many filaments of light. And just as you are only light, so are all of those little roots and flowers, shrubs and trees. They are manifestations of creative power.

The difference between you and them is that you are able to move in consciousness with how you create and they do not necessarily move in consciousness. They move in what may be termed a natural – that is why we say nature – rhythm. Whereas you as a human being have thought faculties to make determinations, flowers do not determine anything. They work with a much more natural rhythm. So as you spend time in the garden, you will be able to see and experience that rhythm and learn to work with it.

You are beginning to perceive that there are benevolent phenomena behind the friendly faces of the flowers, that there are loving realities beyond the range of the retina and that when you are receptive, meaning – that miracle of the multidimensional – may manifest itself outside the tourniquet of language and the constricting muscles of the rational mind. These are all part of a shared consciousness into which each human being can tap. Your inner life is not confined by materiality.

As you are starting to appreciate, your garden can be very beautiful on its own, but with the co-creative process of you as a conscious being working with it and knowing – 'ah, that needs a little space here, that goes there, this color could work here', you are actually learning your relationship to natural creative order. Do you understand?

A lot of your journey in the garden is ... just to get you really here on Earth. You think you've been here, but actually you've been abstracted; you haven't been in your body a lot this lifetime. You're just coming into it at this time, especially through your relationship to the garden.

So let yourself sink completely into that and don't view the process as you merely experiencing the garden. You are actually there experiencing fields of energy. So let yourself go to them. Don't be afraid of where the garden takes you. Because very quickly with just a few deep breaths ... If you will sit there and hold a flower, you are actually able to go into the substance of that flower and become aware. Now if you take that experience, breathing in, you can let yourself go, just as you did see Alice in Wonderland disappear into the woods. Let yourself go into it. And you will see that nature, that grand matrix of creative power, has many things to teach you.

With love and light,
Mother Nature.

13

Cultivating Mystery and Trust

If my garden were a painting, it would be a small naive work, detailed and optimistic. In my early mental conception of it, (for my gardening and plant knowledge were nominal) all I knew was that I wanted to resist the formal structure and planning that had governed so much of my life. There was appeal in unruliness, beauty in asymmetry.

Early evenings, I'd lean over the upper deck railing and, with a bird's eye view, indulgently moon over the crescent-shaped beds, noting how the individual plants were growing, how the plantings overall were beginning to blend and assume their own pleasing pattern, partly planned and partly serendipitous. Sometimes I'd wake early in the morning and envisage a new arrangement which would not only provide better growing conditions for the plants, but also improve the overall aesthetic. Aha! I'd say. Now why didn't I think of that before? But of course we are only ready to 'see' things or to make improvements when we're ready, and not before. Those exciting moments of illumination and rerouting, like all of nature, have their own perfect timings and cannot be hastened or predetermined.

As I learned more about what would grow where, and as my neighbours' trees grew, the proportions of light and shade changed substantially, so that for some months, I *trans*planted as much as planted. Impulsively I created a few pockets of mystery. Rounding a corner you might find a clump of Cape York lilies peeping through the liver-colored stems of tarrow leaves, or a serenely sculpted icon resting inconspicuously under the large flaps of elephant ears, her elegant throat garlanded by variegated ivy. The rear garden was unfenced and backed on to a reserve, the perimeter of which I planted out with dozens of bird-attracting native trees, shrubs and ground cover.[1]

Although my plot was tiny (and also *because* it was), there was a lot to think about, a lot to do. Uncharacteristically, I did not try to do everything at once, mostly because my energy, which had always been prodigious, was low. However, my desire to create a beautiful, sacred space around me was strong. This fortuitous combination of drives led me to undertake the planting in exuberant bursts, which helped me to enjoy the process rather than being focussed on the end result. I found it was wise to have a plan, but foolish to fall in love with it, for as the seasons went by, the seeds and saplings, cuttings and climbers (many given by friends) grew and assumed larger or different shapes than expected.

Thus the garden evolved slowly, experimentally, flexibly into a hickledy-pickledy green life with its own casual charm, colorful outbursts and tranquillity. A living, breathing, changeable mosaic of foliage – serrated, ruffled and smooth mixed with spiky and scratchy, dull and wispy brushed against shiny and broad, speckled and plain merged with striped and splashed, elliptical contrasted with lanceolated, dark with pale – most of its myriad pieces ingeniously found a way to grow which accommodated their neighbours. Those who either overwhelmed or became engulfed by others soon found themselves transplanted to more appropriate territory.

Gertrude Jekyll, whose gardening book *Wood and Garden* was published in 1899 when she was fifty-six and whose writings still impact on today's gardeners, was one of the most famous innovators in garden history. She claimed that 'planting ground is painting a landscape with living things and I hold that good gardening takes rank within the bounds of the fine arts, so I hold that to plant well needs an artist of no mean capacity'.

For me, gardening definitely became not only art, but also, to some considerable degree, invocation. Some days when I was more wilful and narcissistic, I felt myself imposing the plants and my muddling pattern of them, on the earth. Other days, when the energy of the Others blended with mine, the gardening was no less energetic, but it was much less effort. In that exultant, creative flow when I felt myself a deep channel for the community of all beings, felt the sun and the stars singing and dancing through my blood, it seemed I could do anything. I could be Creatrix.

Friends pronounced my thumbs green, but when I emerged from those fragile, finite phases of playing the eminence grise, I was reluctant to assume that badge of merit. Far from being a seasoned gardener, I was an absolute beginner, a bumbling rookie; enthusiastic, yes, and practical in my care, but still pretty green compared with the depth of knowledge and experience acquired by veteran, full-cycle gardeners like my late grandfather. Most of the credit for the growth of my modest plantings I gladly cede to nature – to the living organisms themselves, and their complex and miraculous interactions with the light, the site, the climate and, not least of all, the soil. On our ancient island continent, much of the land is so eroded, degraded, depleted, so *poor* that, as my father likes to say, you wouldn't grow old in it, let alone grow anything else. But in this charmed coastal strand, if you plunge a dead stick into the ground, especially during the rainy season, it's just as likely to sprout and grow.

Hence, I enjoyed some heartening successes, mostly arising from trial and error. Inherent in this modus operandi, naturally, were errors of judgment which led to casualties. Some quickly became apparent; others emerged a season or two later. I under- or overestimated growth rates, heights, widths, the amount of available or required sunlight, or water, or lack of it. But these miscalculations and setbacks didn't deter me. Rather they made the whole co-creative process more fascinating, for they taught me important things – about the plants themselves and their preferences and idiosyncracies, about the earth, the climate, about the creatures (the birds, snakes, water dragons, dragonflies, butterflies, echidnas, possums, bandicoots, bush rats) who came in from the forest, and about the intricate web of interconnectedness among them all. They taught me how much there is to learn about and from nature and how rewarding and beneficial the whole co-creative process can be – for the plants, the creatures and us. Since we're all in this web together, we gardeners in particular may as well help to spin one as universally nourishing and ravishing as we can.

Concurrently, the garden – and gardening – developed into a trove of tropes for me. Like so many gnomes, they lurked about under piles of rotting leaves, in the faces of flowers, in the tilling of the soil, in the rabid regrowth of weeds, in my plodding pursuit of an elusive ideal, in the turning of the compost heap, in the most unlikely and unsalubrious places,

waiting to pop up with their arms full of their buried treasures
– their artful allusions, their florid symbolism, their grand
personifications, their subtle significance or refined figura-
tiveness. My garden, like every garden, became a paragon of
perpetual change and unexpected outcomes. It enticed me to
muse, puzzle or chuckle, to be patient, to loosen the Gordian
knots of control (you can strategically plan, you can plant
till your back seizes and prune till your arms ache, but
ultimately the plants will swell and sprout, mature and fruit,
proliferate and present themselves in their own individual
rhythms and configurations) and to stay flexible, to remain
receptive to fresh or unscheduled insights, consequences.

Joseph Campbell reckoned that life could be read in terms
of prose – *de*notation – or poetry – *co*notation. For me, being
in the garden was, as often as not, threaded, studded,
overlayed, highlighted and generally engorged with poetry,
not all of it a panegyric. Batting away the blood-sucking
mosquitoes who wanted to pierce a piece of me or ripping out
the lantana that threatened to smother the native saplings,
carried as much allegorical weight as, say, the replenishing
pleasure of twilight watering.

Planting and pruning, watching and watering, composting
and fertilising, I felt as if I were discovering the emerging
pattern of both the garden and my own life through uncovering,
rather than imposing a form on either. One day I'd feel
diffident, the next I'd dig and heave, tote and plant with
bravura, and the energy somehow stuck to the garden (as oil
will to canvas) and beamed out at the beholder. Many gardening
writers are full of mundane how-to advice (and this, unquestionably, serves a purpose) but I was learning to count as
much on attitude, state of mind and receptivity as on technique.
I exchanged how-to tips with gardening pals and read a few

books, but mostly I kept my senses, my intuition, call it what you will, tuned to Deva-FM for their transmissions, for I had no wish to suck the marrow from the magic.

In the process, I learned that you don't need a lump of land the size of Sissinghurst[2] to create a beautiful home garden. One woman I read about spent three years thinking about how 'to make a small scale country garden with trees, climbers, shrubs, soft fruits, herbs, vegetables, perennial and annual flowers'. After wrestling with the space and climatic problems involved and despite the feedback of gardening experts who considered her an eccentric, she resolutely set about realising her cherished dream – on the topmost, twenty-third floor of a council tower block in east London!

As my garden grew, I marvelled at how, despite their infinite array of form, textures and hues, their divergent requirements for growth and the propinquity in which they suddenly or gradually found themselves, they mostly co-existed companionably and harmoniously; how they created their own inter-connected balance and, with a little help from me, thrived. Some established themselves by putting down deep central roots; right alongside them other types secured themselves with shallow spreading roots. Some scattered their delicately veined foliage low and wide across the soil, others grew to imposing heights, providing protection for the more fragile. Some were subdued blenders, happy to lurk in the shade, providing an unobtrusive but solid background against which the showier varieties made bright counter-points in fuller sun. Some were vigorous growers, others took their time. Some distinguished themselves through fragrance, others through their blooms. Down in the burgeoning micro-rainforest, however, relations weren't always so civil and supportive. If the inner garden took shape and flourished under my benevolent despotism, the rainforest grew up virtually as a laissez faire regime. It was a case of every tree, shrub and vine for itself as they limbered, spread, crept and coiled themselves up, up through the densening canopy towards the light. That propensity, it appeared, was a definite demonstration of consciousness. As I said, tropes, tropes everywhere.

Anticipating and tending the needs of the plants in an increasingly familiar and intimate way, I became emotionally and energetically entangled in their various life cycles. I actively assisted and delighted in their growth spurts and bloomings, diagnosed and treated their ailments, monitored their dormancy, mourned their untimely demises and despatched them to that steaming departure lounge of the gardening world, the compost heap, there to break down in aid of nourishing their successors.

Of course there was nothing revolutionary in this constant caring nexus. It merely enlisted me in the long, long line of those for whom the apparently ordinary practice of gardening becomes an intriguing interplay of elements both earthy and ethereal, a constant challenge to co-create, a regular cause for celebration, a numinous joy.

My Dear Child,

I am delighted that you are discovering through your garden your natural fellowship with nature. Nature is neither structured nor symmetrical. The asymmetrical has, as you perceive, its own special beauty, and it also signals change and growth, movement and evolution.

90

I notice that some of that tranquillity you are co-creating with the devic queendom is rubbing off on you. I also notice that your garden is constantly engaging your imagination, for you think about the plants and the earth not only as you work with them in their natural rhythm, but also in your dreamings of the times ahead. In return, does your garden not please and succour you with its growth and glory, with the creatures it attracts, with the fresh foods it offers up for your plate? And so you are learning about the reciprocal nurturing that happens when you become a co-creator with the earth.

As your garden blooms, so does your inner being, for you are starting to experience the wondrous reality that all growing things, including human beings, make up one seamless yet complex assembly or, as your ecologists like to say, web of life. This web, despite its unpredictability and turbulence at times, is ultimately benign.

In the digging and sifting, mulching and fertilising, weeding and pruning, you are cultivating more than the garden. You are cultivating your soul, for the two are inseparable rites of passage.

The creative energy you direct to the garden right now is really just one way of expressing your passion for life. Through this expression, you are learning to create for the sheer joy of creating, as I do. I do not struggle to have human beings acknowledge or understand me and my creations. If they choose to understand, they will.

Through your relationship with the garden, you will be able, if you will allow yourself, if you will

trust the process, to experience a profound letting go
– of the constraints and pressures of linear time (a
mere fabrication of your rational world), of many of
your ingrained and habitual fears, of the rigidity of
the 'shoulds' and 'oughts' that have governed so
much of your life.

And as you admire the uncountable permutations
of life and their inherent inter-relatedness and equilibrium in what is, after all, a very small space, you
will begin to experience a deep knowing, a certainty
that rests outside the realms of logic and empirical
comprehension, that life also unfolds impeccably in
and beyond your beloved mini-cosmos.

In this deeper trust that comes from what you are
seeing in the garden – because you are seeing how
everything really perfectly fits together – you will be
able to heal all that fear in your heart, the doubt that
life in your larger world will work. And that is the
healing that is coming now for you. And this is really
what your writing is to be about. Helping people to
understand that everything is designed to work
perfectly, that nothing is failure, everything is
accomplishment, everything is purposeful, no matter
what feelings you have about it.

Even your unhappiness is worth loving, for it heralds
your readiness for change. Painful feelings and experiences are simply another segment of this life.

Thorn on the rose. Is it painful? Or is it just there?
It is really just an energy field. It can be painful. But it
doesn't have to be. If you will learn to hold the rose
where the thorns are not, you do not feel pain from the
thorn on the rose. And the rose actually gets to

blossom, for it is one of the highest vibrations in your world. That, by the way, is why it is so revered by all. The rose is a frequency of energy that is highly refined. The thorns are there to keep that refined energy field from being eaten by other things. It is a wonderful energy, the rose.

My child, your journey in the garden is a magical one. Embrace it with an open heart and it will take you to places you have never been before.

With love and light,

Mother Nature.

1. The forest plantings included: Atherton palm (*Laccospadix australasica*), Bangalow palm (*Archontophoenix cunninghamiana*), Bernie's Tamarind (*Diploglottus Bernieana*), black apple (*Planchonella australis*), black bean (*Castanospermum australe*), black booyong (*Argyrodendron actinophyllum*), bracelet honey myrtle (*M. armillaris*), broad-leaved palm lily (*Cordyline petiolaris*), cabbage palm (*Livistona australis*), Carpentaria palm (*Carpentaria acuminata*), cheese tree (*Glochidion ferdinandii*), creek cherry (*Syzygium australe*), creek sandpaper fig (*Ficus coronata*), Cudgerie (*Flindersia schottiana*), Davidson's plum (*Davidsonia pruriens var. jerseyana*), dwarf palm lily (*Cordyline haageana*), elephant ears (*Cunjevoi Brisbanensis*), fairy paintbrushes (*Archidendron grandiflorum*), Queensland fan palm (*Livistona benthamii*), fine-leaved tuckeroo (*Lepiderema pulcherimma*), Finlay's silky oak (*Grevillea baileyana*), flame tree (*Brachychiton acerfolius*), golden penda (*Xanthostemon chrysanthus*), kadamba (*Anthocephalus chinensis*), lemon myrtle (*Backhousia citriadoro*), Lomatia silkyoak (*Lomatia fraxinofolia*), elephant's ears/native cunjevoi (*Alocasia Brisbanensis*), native frangipani (*Hymenosporum flavum*), native gardenia (*Randia benthamiana*), native guava (*Rhodomyrtus psidiodes*), native lassiandra (*Melastoma affine*), Nightcap wattle (*Acacia orites*), pencil cedar (*Polyscias murrayi*), pink euodia (*Euodia elleryana*), pleated ginger Booroogum (*Alpinia Arctiflora*), powder puff lilli pilly (*Syzygium Wilsonii*), Queensland fan palm (*Licuala ramseyii*), Queensland maple (*Flindersia brayleana*), red carrabeen (*Geissois benthamii*), red-fruited palm lily (*Cordyline rubra*), red kamala (*Mallotus philippensis*), riberry (*Syzygium leuhmannii*), scaly tree fern (*Cyathea cooperi*), solitaire palm (*Ptychosperma elegans*), tuckeroo (*Cupaniopsis anacardioides*), water gum (*Syzygium francissi*), white oak (*Grevillea hilliana*), yellow wood (*Sarcomelicope simplicifolia*).
2. The English estate on which Vita Sackville-West (1892-1962), poet, novelist and gardener, created a legendary garden.

14
____

Meeting a Monarch

While training a Guinea gold vine along the fence early one morning, I heard a soft thud against one of the living room's glass doors. A small bird I hadn't seen before was crouched, still and dazed on the deck. From behind, it looked an undistinguished grey. Hastily I filled a shallow lid with sugared water and, moving as slowly and smoothly as possible, I knelt down about eighteen inches from it. Its eyes were half closed and unfocussed and it seemed to be barely breathing.

Putting my attention on my heart centre, I beamed love to the little creature which, I now saw, had an exquisite, rusty orange chest, short black whiskers, twiggy, leaden-blue legs and a face like a wise old professor. Within a minute, the bird appeared to breathe more deeply. The urge to comfort it by touch was irresistible. Tentatively, almost imperceptibly, I glided my hand behind it and with a touch I hoped would feel as light and tender as one of its own dear feathers, I stroked the very tip of its white-edged tail with my index finger. The bird opened and closed its beak a few times, opened its eyes wide, then closed them and tilted its head slightly back in what appeared to be a posture of surrender.

We stayed like that for another couple of minutes – one extending a caring touch, the other sedately compliant. When the bird finally opened its eyes with complete focus, I slowly withdrew my hand and sat absolutely still. We looked at each other for several seconds and then, wide-eyed with surprise to find himself or herself (it was hard to tell, as the sexes look alike) in such close proximity to a human, my tiny friend took off in a colorful flash and a gentle flurry of feathers. I went inside and discovered from my bird book that I'd just had an encounter with a spectacled monarch.

Thoreau[1] wrote of a similar encounter: 'I once had a sparrow alight upon my shoulder for a moment while I was hoeing in a village garden, and I felt I was more distinguished by that circumstance than I should have been by any epaulette I could have worn'. I knew just how he felt.

In *Bird Life*, Ian Rowley explains: 'The language of birds … consists of vocal and visual displays given either separately or in combination. Avian communication consists of conveying the intention or mood of one individual to others. It is helpful here to consider our own species, although this is sometimes a dangerous thing to do if carried too far. Consider how much information can be conveyed from one person to another without the use of words. Our eyes are possibly the most expressive parts of our bodies and they can show affection, hate or fear, depending on the dilation of the pupil and the amount of iris exposed. Scowling, smiling and yawning all convey mood without the need for talking. Confidence or insecurity may be shown in the way we stand and walk. So birds convey how they are feeling to other birds, and to many people a most fascinating aspect of bird study is the unravelling of bird language.'

My Dear Child,

There will be times when, just like your tiny feathered friend, you will try to surge forward on your merry or wilful way because there appears to be an exciting opening ahead of you, because the outlook appears bright and clear. That there will be invisible 'walls' ahead is a necessary and inevitable fact of life. These walls may pull you up short, cause you pain and suffering and require you to rethink your manner of approach, your flight path, your pace, your motivation or your proposed arrival time at the next point along your life's journey. These 'walls' may delay or detour you or cause you to change your plans entirely.

When such difficulties arise, do not lose heart. Have faith in the greater wisdom and underlying order of nature, for you are always being guided – sometimes imperceptibly and sometimes most glaringly – along the serpentine stream of your own highly individual life story. The Divine resides in every moment, in every breath, every blink of the questing eye. You just have to remember to look for it.

When you hit a 'wall' – of resistance, of loss, of betrayal, of circumstance, of bad health, or whatever – it may seem unjust, unwarranted, undeserved. It may knock you dizzy for a while; it may even immobilise you. However, seen in a different light, through a shift in your own perception, these 'walls' are not obstructive barriers; they are instructive guideposts sagely re-routing your path ahead and providing opportunities for increased awareness, for change, sometimes for forgiveness and compassion for yourself as well as for others.

Through such experiences, you may begin to perceive, piece by piece the larger picture of what is truly possible for you to achieve in this lifetime. When you understand that your human trials are the means of preparing you for your own future, you can stop frittering your thoughts and feelings, your energy and actions on the unattainable, the impossible or the insoluble, and redirect them to those areas and activities through which it is possible for you to achieve.

When you do hit a wall and it leaves you feeling winded or wounded, confused or lost along your way, remember the wisdom of your little bird friend. Do not try to keep flying, to soar above the painful things that are happening to you. Stop, put your feet on the earth, or, if you can, sit or lie on it. Pause. Breathe. Bring your awareness back into your body. Let the earth's healing power help you to ground and centre yourself.

It is not always in your best interests to 'cope' with adversity. To cope can mean to deal competently with a situation or problem; but 'cope' also means to meet in battle. In your world, words, over time, assume their own flavours and emotional charges, and 'coping' seems to have acquired a slightly depressing air. It does indeed give the impression of embattlement. In your modern lingo, 'cope' is a verb, an action or doing word. This is hardly surprising, for you live in a time where doing, like coping, is endemic and addictive. For many of you, coping has become synonymous with doing, acting, working, keeping busy and on the move. These are all behaviours your society holds in high esteem. And of course, in moderation, in balance, action and mobility are essential in your physical world. But when you cling to a mechanistic, fix-up-the-outside, ignore-the-inside mentality, you lose the holy art of how to simply be. And it is your beingness, not your doingness, your feelings, not your thoughts that connect you to the inner realities from which all true answers and new possibilities flow.

Did you know that in bygone centuries, before people were sending frantic faxes or nattering on the Net, 'cope' was not a verb? It was a noun, the name of something. In mediaeval times, 'cope' had an ecclesiastical meaning; it was a long ceremonial cloak worn in religious processions. 'Cope' also had a poetic meaning. It meant ... the vault of heaven! 'Coping' seldom has a poetic or spiritual meaning for people today.

When the going gets tough and you're in the full flight of your own coping strategies, how much poetry do you feel? How often do you experience the vault of heaven when you're coping with the now? How much spontaneity do you feel when you're coping with the now? How often do you sacrifice spontaneity for efficient management, or obligation or guilt? How often do you defer sadness or rest, rage or even happiness by not being in the now? Can you allow a telephone to ring unanswered? How often do seemingly urgent matters in the now relate to the expectations of others? How often do you oblige by coping on demand? Have you ever lain on a massage table and, while the masseur dug their skilful, kind hands into the pain in your body, put your mind to work on what you'll cook for dinner?

How often do you miss the moment because your mind is preoccupied with what upset you yesterday or what could go wrong tomorrow? Sometimes, I notice, you're 'coping' so well with life's vicissitudes, you don't even know you're in pain.

Allow yourself to acknowledge and express your hurt (even if only to yourself and to the cosmos), no matter how great its depth. Take the time to gather in your energies which can, under pressure, become as scattered as wheat seeds in the wind.

In times of trouble, try stepping aside and watching, with compassion and without judgement, the frantic ferris wheel of thoughts that circle through your mind. Do not try to stop the thoughts and feelings, but at the same time try not to let yourself be swept away by joy or smothered by sadness. Strive to see beyond these fluctuations, to recognise the deeper state of being which underpins all of them and temporal experience.

If you can truly allow yourself to accept the pain rather than resisting it, you will, like your royal little friend, more rapidly reach its exquisite centre. And when you do, your physical and etheric bodies will not contract so intensely. Your acceptance of the pain will assist them to expand and become more luminous. This is also the space in which help, sometimes miraculous in its manifestation, can be given.

Help can come in the most unlikely form, from the most unexpected sources. And there is deep healing in its mere proffering, as your bespectacled friend did discover when he accepted your transmission of love. Love and compassion effortlessly cross the boundaries of speech and species, of visible and invisible. Remember, all you need to do is ask: Please help me.

With love and light,
Mother Nature.

1. American poet and essayist Henry David Thoreau (1817-62) built and moved into a cabin he built by Walden Pond, Concord Massachusetts where he lived alone ('45-'47) 'thinking, observing nature and growing his own food (mostly beans)'. His masterwork *Walden*: or *Life in the Woods* (1854) records his solitary happiness.

15

____

Under the Canopy

Sitting on the step one morn,
deep in the shadow of lack;
lightness leached from every bone.
Time to go planting out the back.

Down the gully, wretched, hot,
stamping out my fear,
ferrying a tray of pots
towards the conch of Nature's ear.

Among the spiralling life I paced
andante as I toiled.
Each shoot tenderly I placed
in the edaphic peace of soil.

A wagtail hopped beside my thigh
and gave me quite a start.
'Sweet, pretty creature!' he cried,
and landed on my songless heart.

In that elastic, timeless weave
I lost and found myself,
not alone as I'd believed,
but counterpart to Earth's vast wealth.

Perception's veil began to tear
there on the forest floor.
Naked need allowed me to hear
the rustling wisdom of Her lore:

'Expectation's silvery bend
can build a mazy web.
You shape your life as you intend,
So trust its course, its flow and ebb.

'Remember, grace cannot be seized,
though sometimes it descends
when you're ready to receive
from unanticipated friends.'

And so I offered up my face
To that lush world of green
and, grateful, breathed in the grace
of allies near, beloved, unseen.

16

Light Moves

Intent on the earth, planting seedlings of parsley, rocket and sweet basil, I might not have noticed that special small creature poised just above my head. But a glint of light on its fine wings caught my eye.

It hovered in that spot long enough for me to take in the outstanding details of its unique form. Its two sets of gilded, gossamer wings shimmered magnificently in the mid-morning sun; its massive eyes virtually covered its head. Then off it zoomed, riveting my attention as it performed a series of stunning aerobatics, scooping up smaller insects as it hawked a regular beat through the garden. For minutes, I watched, hypnotised, looking and looking until my eyes watered from squinting into the blazing summer light. Then as instantly as it had appeared, the little, golden apparition sped back into the forest.

All that season and into the autumn, the dragonflies came in from the wetlands in the rear forest to hunt for food in my garden. I was always pleased to see them energetically devouring lots of mosquitoes and flies on their speedy manoeuvres (they can fly up to fifty kilometres an hour). Of course, dragonflies were not born the sheer, golden light creatures I saw whizzing among my plants. Each one evolves into a glistening miracle of beauty through a series of metamorphoses.

Dragonflies live near freshwater ponds, rivers or creeks. Each dragonfly begins its life journey as a 'nymph' which hatches from the eggs the mother dragonfly lays either in water or on the stems of water plants. 'Nymphs' are dull brown, sluggish, ugly creatures known to trout fishermen as 'mud eyes'. They have thick bodies, large heads and a savage-looking lower lip with pincers on the end. Nymphs live in water for a year or more, growing and moulting, shedding several skins before turning into dragonflies.

Catching sight of the dragonfly in that morning light prompted me to revisit one of my favourite books, *About Time*. The book's cover features a hologram of a nautilus shell, an image which is visible only when the book is held in a certain light. Until then, the shell looks like a square of silvery plastic; it exists only in potential as an invisible swirl of submerged light frequencies. The book mentions David Bohm, a physicist who has proposed an underlying reality in the universe which he has called the Implicate Order. Like a hologram, this is 'a realm of frequencies and potentialities that underlies our illusion of concreteness'. Bohm and the brain-scientist Karl Pribram have speculated that 'the illusion of concreteness that consciousness gives us – our manifest reality of feelings, perceptions and life processes – might be formed by the interference patterns created between our holographic beings with each other and the holographic universe'. Bohm contends that 'each person enfolds something of the spirit of the other in his consciousness'.

My Dear Child,

The dragonflies are little spirit beings that are also a very important part of the creative matrix that you are learning about.

Whenever you behold a dragonfly, remember that human beings, too, are continually evolving their bodies and their consciousness.

Within this life that you are now experiencing, on this endlessly moving footway of evolution, you, too, will pass through many forms, physically, mentally, emotionally and spiritually. Above all, it is the evolution of your soul which will bring you into the fullness of your own individual truth and beauty. The gold that you so admire in the dragonfly's wings is the symbolic color of the soul and represents its alchemical power to transmute your being.

Like the dragonfly, you, too, are just light, vibrating at various levels, according to your consciousness. As you lift up your golden-winged spirit towards higher levels of understanding and service on your planet, you will naturally draw towards you more beauty, harmony and joy.

Nature is an energy field of ceaseless transformations and, as you are an integral part of nature, you will, throughout your life, be given the opportunity to grow and shed many 'skins'. You may shed some of the skins of competing, of striving and over-ambition;

you may shed the skins of financial security and material possessions; you may shed some of the skins of the ego, your image of yourself. Over time, you may jettison some or all of your social connections, your political, spiritual beliefs. Finally, through death in old age, you will shed the physical body itself.

You may also shed some of the thickened skins of your conditioned fears, your accumulated griefs, regrets and resentments, your need for others' approval; you may slough off the identifying skins of one or many occupations. For I see that you still cling to the tissue of illusion that what you do for a living in your world of matter determines who you are – and of what value. Does the dragonfly stake its identity, value and place on the number of insects caught in a day, or on the distance it flies before the closing of the flowers at nightfall? You may learn a lot and find a great measure of personal fulfilment through following those worldly pursuits that attract you, but remember: the truth of who you are does not depend on your worldly function. Worldly activities can be a carapace that appears to offer security or permanence or protection, but which can distract you from experiencing the expansiveness of your inner being.

Psychic shedding or transforming often entails altering or being altered radically in your form or function. It involves being true to your soul; it involves letting yourself discover the unvarnished truth of your being. It involves converting, sometimes arduously, astringently, from one form into another. This may require your going into a dark place of not knowing, and remaining there for as long as it takes for your new self to materialise.

When you do this, many skins will automatically begin to fall away. During such phases, friends and relations, accustomed to relating to you on more exterior levels, may become impatient with you; they may be confounded or cranky about your inwardness, which, to them, may appear dull, self-indulgent, a cop-out. Your society neither understands nor supports conscious solitude and contemplation. It tends to be viewed as a dysfunctional retreat from 'the real world' and not as the penetrating adventure in the other 'real worlds' it can be.

Those who find your chosen introspection most confronting may proffer their own projected remedies. They may offer to take you places, to introduce you to new people, to buy you (if you live alone) a pet; they may suggest you try nattering on the Net or taking up an active hobby or a new line of work. They may see your introspection (even if you are living in a partnership) as rejection, not selection; or as failure, not fortitude. They would find it easier to understand if you sojourned for a week or so at, say, an Eastern religious retreat, for that at least is a finite term of spiritual experience legitimised by tradition, orthodoxy and a hint of the exotic. My child, your retreat is your private affair. Whether you create it by moving to a foreign country or remaining in the privacy of your own home is a matter of personal choice. Once you've set it up, remember you require no one's approval to withdraw to it.

Those who do not understand or accept this are the ones who could not bear the prospect of the torments of transformation that go on inside the sluggish swamps of *being* with yourself. Yet if you are to continue to grow and change in this life, it is essential at times to venture into those swamps. The path through that murky terrain is the road less travelled, but the most direct one to true personal growth. It is only through such growth that you become freer, lighter, that you can ultimately emerge golden-winged, airborne, beautiful, with a broader vision of life.

When you are deeply withdrawn in your transformation, people may assume you are doing nothing or that you are seriously 'depressed', (that pejorative coverall bandied about so casually in your society by those too fearful to experience the transformative powers of consciously connecting with grief). They may assume that you have 'dropped your bundle' (which, in effect, is what transformation is about – shedding the baggage of your past which has weighed you down). They may urge you to 'loosen up', to go out more, *do* more. This is when you need to trust and believe in your own inner process, no matter how uneventful your outer life appears – to others or to yourself.

At times, your own interior voices will insist you 'get a grip', 'stop wasting time', 'get out there' and 'do something'. But you are only ready to do something new, love a new somebody or love somebody anew, when you have gone through the metamorphosis that helps you reach a more authentic layer of yourself. Growing from a 'mudeye' into a new creature with superior vision takes time, so let yourself take the time it requires to complete this phase. If you try to wrest yourself from the darkness, from the painful throbbing and churning of your cocoon too early, you will emerge messy, mangled, a creature half-formed, neither one thing nor the other.

And even when the process is complete and you are reborn, your new contours may be a mere outline against the startling light of day. Be satisfied with that. Be patient. Trust that your full form, color and fine details, will, in time, be filled in and that your new way of contributing to nature's web will present itself.

So whenever you see a dragonfly, take heart that the hard work of self-transformation has its rewards.

Sit quietly now, close your eyes and breathe in gold light. With each breath, allow yourself to feel that you are a being of light. Your body is a beautiful vibrational energy field. It is not heavy and it is not thick. It is just vibrating energy. Your body, your mind, your feelings ... all of these are only vibrating light.

Allow your mind to slow down and your emotions to be at peace. As you breathe, begin to be aware that the vibration of the body extends far beyond the physical form. As you breathe, you can start to feel the etheric body. It is a beautiful body of light which, like the physical body, is also just a form. It is composed of countless fibres of light that reach way out into space.

Feel yourself suspended in light, glorious light.

Ask for help in letting go of whatever or whoever does not serve your highest good.

Then slowly bring your awareness back into your body and open your eyes.

With love and light,

Mother Nature.

17

Moonshadow

One summer was dry, ultra-dry. Day after pitiless day the air was heavy, not only with humidity, but with the conversational weight of words attempting to explain the discomfiting weather – 'Greenhouse', 'El Nino', 'Deforestation', 'Ozone depletion'.

Beachcombing at dusk, however, always holds the possibility of an activating breeze and an eye-salving sky of pink or purple. Down towards the ocean one evening, a young man with a friendly, freckled face and a shock of carrot-colored hair, was setting up a large telescope, aimed, it appeared, at the moon.

'Is it a special night? An eclipse or something?' I inquired.

'Every night is a special night,' he replied, with a smile. 'Would you like a look?'

Squinting through the telescope's mighty eye, I glimpsed a chrome-tinted moon, crusted, shadowed, pitted and revolving fast.

'I think you're looking at the Sea of Rains,' the young man said.

'Whoever named the moonscape had a poet's heart, didn't they?' I replied, citing some favourites from the far side –

Sea of Nectar, Sea of Serenity, Sea of Vapours, Sea of Crises, Seething Bay, Ocean of Storms, Marsh of Decay, Marsh of Sleep. Oppenheimer Crater could do with renaming, but on the near side, how about Foaming Sea, Dante Crater, Icarus Crater or Lake of Dreams for pure poetry about a planet that has no air, wind, water or life that we recognise? Still, to the naked or telescopic eye, it was eerily beautiful.

'Saturn's quite something, too,' the young man assured me. I thanked him for the viewing and went on my way.

*   *   *

Later, in the small hours, it was too hot to sleep, so I wrapped on a sarong and went outside to watch the play of moonlight on my back garden. In silhouette, the glossy cunjevoi leaves gleamed like giant green ears receiving celestial signals. A whiff of breeze stirred the upper branches of the silvery banksia, tilting its leaves to form a lacy constellation of metallic glints. But otherwise all was still.

The scents of gardenia and native ginger wavered in the air. I swished my way through the curtain of rear boundary foliage into the forest and sat down on a patch of molasses grass among the young wattles and velvet leaf bushes. The previous day a Clarence River roughskin snake had slithered into my neighbour's pantry, and two days before that when I was watering the cabbage palms in the gully, I'd accidentally disturbed a four-metre diamond python sunning itself among the decaying leaf cover. Barely any light penetrated the canopy that night, but that was fine by me. I wanted to venture into the dark, to feel the pulse of the earth, even if that entailed a bit of risk in a dim grove.

Under the canopy, time was fluid and expansive, punctuated only by intermittent rustlings, slow-moving moonbeams and the occasional call of a tawny frogmouth or a willie wagtail. The wagtails, I'd noticed, often sang when the moon was full. One night, I'd even seen one singing under a street light. The night music of the forest did not disturb the enveloping hush, but rather augmented it. And I, at last, wished to court rather than counteract the silence, was ready to listen, without prejudice, to the messages that it might deliver. I was learning that to commune deeply with the ineffable – that formless, faceless, genderless reality – you have to turn away for a while from the color and movement of the outer world and invite yourself in to the silence and the dark; to dance a while there with your daemons. When I first entered those realms, I found myself in what appeared to be an empty wasteland. To my fearful and unacculturated eye, the terrain initially appeared hostile – featureless, lifeless, lacking as it did any physical incident, movement, detail or obvious markers of personal progress, and making, as it did, a parlous impact on my finances. But the longer I spent there, the more I trusted and sank into that mysterious interior landscape, the more compelling and sustaining I found it. Through retreat, patience and prayer, I began to divine its hidden wells and secret fruits and they sustained me until I was ready to return to the full glare of the exterior world.

I heard the sundering of the sea and decided to return to the beach. The tide was in and the sand squished cool and creamy between my toes as I ambled along. The surf roared and thrashed, its breakers unfurling like phosphorescent satin ribbons, and I felt, as I always do in the presence of that great mother, that I could cast my burdens onto her – and let them peptize in her vast saline solution.

The gibbous moon, her white face partly veiled, threw pale spears of light onto the mercury sea. The sprinkling of lights that defined the caravan park in the far, black distance were repeated and multiplied in the resplendent stars above. Diaphanous clouds rippled across the night sky, echoing the pattern of the nacreous shoreline. Dozens of mini-craters, the size of large dingy coins, pocked the luminous surface of the sand. When the little ghost crabs emerged and scurried about, they were translucent as the moonshine. As above, so below. What kind of alchemy was going on here? Which planet was I on? Talk about walking on the 'floor of heaven'.

There was strong competition for my carousing eye: the moon hastened on her elliptical orbit and every fifteen seconds, the lighthouse (Australia's most powerful, visible at sea for twenty-six nautical miles) did its own flashy revolution, sweeping the land and waters. That beloved national icon, that monumental evocator of the natural law that light, inevitably is followed by shadow, 'the other side of the Creator', as C.G. Jung called it, is one of the few constants around here, I mused, as it held me alternately transfixed by its projective shafts and reprieved by the noble slabs of darkness in their wake.

My Dear Child,

I bring you some reflections from the heraldic night sky, for I see you are under the spell of the light, yet succoured by the shadows.

In your modern times, the psychic shadow – the other side of human nature – has been relegated so effectively to the unconscious seams of your psyches that, lacking rituals to acknowledge and incorporate it, most people don't even begin to uncover it until midlife. That's when the tectonic plates of your underworld start grinding with such force that they heave the shadow up to the surface, shaking your life up in any number of ways – as a dissolution of ideals, as a shattering of self-image, as descents into the ashes of regret, as feelings of being footloose or rudderless, as indefinable longing for something 'other'.

The shadows of your personalities come in many guises – arrogance, dependency, selfishness, jealousy, greed, impatience, laziness, obsession, pessimism, competitiveness, cowardice, pettiness, greed ... As long as such qualities are ignored by you, they can rear up unexpectedly and indirectly as physical or psychological ailments, in shocking or upsetting incidents, as moodiness, apathy, hurtful behaviour, forgetfulness, to name a few outlets. Which explains why so many people are terrified of the unconscious.

In your times, the value of the psyche's shadow has been diminished, given what you might call some bad press and sent even further underground. The honouring of your shady sides has been smothered by the showy kisses of unremitting goodness and light. You've been told that if you use your mind in the right way, eat the right foods, utter the right words, send out the right vibes, there is nothing you cannot accomplish, that you can do and have it all, that you can – and indeed should – live endlessly in the light.

But as is evident all around you, life, for all its overarching beauty and power, has its limitations. Real spiritual maturity recognises this and bows to those invincible necessities which present themselves as exercises in humility and acceptance.

You are the soul infusing the personality; you are the personality, soul-infused. Living within this paradigm, ruptures and splits in your human relations are inevitable. When they do occur, there is usually a big soul lesson going on. If you can locate and pay some attention to the banished aspect of you that is trying to burst forth into the light; if you can accept it as an integral (albeit unappealing) part of who you are, it may not need to reassert itself in such a disruptive way in future. When you shine a light on your own unrecognised impulses, you will lessen the possibility of these popping up as 'projections' on to people around you. The thoughts you regard as negative are not the problem; the problem is your fear and denial of them.

For the most part, I see you acting like those delicate, sweet-scented heliotropes in your garden – shunning the shadows, turning your face all day to follow the sun. Have you not just been enjoying the many plants that thrive in the shade of that forest? I have watched you lovingly tending and admiring them for months, for you value them as a vital part of the contrasting beauty of your garden. Likewise, your personal shadow holds great gifts in the form of unrealised potential. Talents and qualities such as spontaneity, creativity, daring, or humour in some beings have been repressed since childhood.

Contacting and expressing these attributes can be an even bigger challenge than owning your so-called darker drives.

Do you wonder why you find the moon and the stars so entrancing? It is because they speak to the deep feminine principle in all beings. They speak not to the hard-edged logic and abstract theories of your sunny mind, but to the fluid perception and poetry of your inner landscape, to the slow, magical revelations of your soul, to the wisdom born of your own torments and anguish.

The moonlight vision that comes from plugging into your intuition, your dreams and your psychic energy offers another way of perceiving life. This vision sees the universe as a timeless play of swirling energies, including good and evil, in eternal flux. It recalls a time when time was cyclical, not linear, yet it does not shy from facing the ever-turbulent sub-atomic reality of the here and now. This way of 'seeing' rather than looking, reveres the consciousness in all of nature, including the darkness. After all, you were conceived and gestated in darkness, and it is darkness which characterises much of space. The moon and stars allude to some of the greatest secrets and most absorbing questions about existence. They remind you that you are one tiny but essential beat in the endless cosmic rhythm. This feminine field of perception, long the domain of the Earth's artists and poets, is rapidly becoming the territory of your scientists who, more and more, find themselves trying to account for phenomena that occur outside their range of causal understanding.

This feminine way of seeing also calls forth rituals which honour humanity's collective unconscious shadow and it promotes behaviours congruent with preserving the Earth. Yet so many of you have 'civilised' yourself to the point where you have lost the ability to relate to nature's mystical cycles, symbols and occurrences – the very things which gave 'primitive' people so much meaning in their lives. Ancient peoples understood very well that they were an inherent motif in the magic carpet weave of life on Earth, but not its centrepiece, and certainly not the sole weavers of its intricate pattern.

In your lifetime, rationalism, materialism, intellect, analysis, science and technology in their unchecked ascendancy, have eclipsed intuition and the poetic faculties of feeling and emotion. They have impeded the instinctive process of your own development and, ipso facto, the Earth's. This is most evident in the juggernaut of your industrial age and the unconscionable way it has violated nature, poisoning the air and waters, despoiling the land.

The deep fissures of darkness in the planetary picture can be overwhelming, so instead of focussing only on what's wrong 'out there', I suggest you also direct your lines of inquiry towards transforming your own inner space, for if you cannot change yourself, you cannot change the world, either. It is not only a case of 'as above, so below', but also 'as within, so without'.

You could begin tonight with a simple ritual to honour your own hidden impulses, for it is only when you start to claim them that you can increase your conscious choice about how you behave. The more choice you acquire, the more you can consciously create the type of world you want to live in.

With love and light,
Mother Nature.

Scanning the shoreline for materials, I picked up a handful of pale shells, some ribbed and smooth, some fan-shaped or purple-lined, others sea-polished or brittle. These I arranged in a small pile on the dry sand. Then I collected a handful of the black basalt stones that proliferate on the local beaches. (For some unexplained reason a small proportion of these are always heart-shaped.) With these stones I formed an adjacent mound.

In the sand, I drew one circle around the pale shells and a second circle (which intersected slightly with the first) around the stones. Kneeling on the sand, I cupped one hand over each pile. I closed my eyes and asked for each pile – the light and the dark – to be blessed and for the two to be integrated. Then I opened my eyes, carefully removed a few of the stones and shells and placed them together in the sliver of intersection between the two circles.

I sat back on my haunches and surveyed my rudimentary handiwork, lying like a sensate promise on the sand. The clouds parted and a pallid draught of moonlight drenched my face. The gravitas of the moon was strong, but I had concluded my business with her for the moment and felt ready for sleep. I took one of the stones with me, warming it in my palm on the way home. A reminder to harvest my lunar wisdom, to invoke and befriend the dark places within, for if you focus on any shadow for long enough 'it tends to grow light'.

18

Ex Libris

Mother Nature does not always send me long messages. Sometimes I have to rush to write down the snippets, notes, postcards and even (good grief) singing telegrams that She delivers to my ear. The quieter I am, the more Her messages come through.

What a writer does with all this privacy, quiet and time is a mystery to those who live and earn their daily bread in more outer-worldly pursuits, and to those who never slow down to a gallop. In the goldfish bowl of small-town life, where gossip is the main sport, the writing life can become a target of relentless curiosity. This Need to Know, this stickybeaking, seems to be in inverse proportion to the degree of intimacy one shares with the inquirer.

'What are you doing?' they will ask. 'You must be doing something!' Scratch this ploy and you uncover the hidden meaning behind its accusation: we don't have enough information on you. On the other hand, one of the ironic sureties in small-town life is that even when you don't know what you're doing, someone else does.

'What are you working on?'

'My consciousness,' is a succinct, truthful answer to the most nosy types.

'Where have you been?'

I'm inclined to reply that I've been in bed having passionate intercourse with Mr Collins, a big dictionary, if ever I saw one. In a film, a male record company executive quipped to a female songwriter whose inspiration was stymied. 'Look around you. There is pain everywhere.' True, no doubt. But equally, the world is full of poetry and a stack of it is lurking in the dictionary.

Confidentially, I do wonder sometimes what I've done with the days. The tide comes in; the tide goes out. The seasons cycle by. I go walkabout a lot and garden. I cook. I birdwatch. In late winter, I watch for the return of the chestnut-breasted mannikins, who cascade from the native holly tree. To get the seed I leave for them, the mannikins scramble about the plate; they jump on each others' backs until they resemble a football scrum.

Come late winter or early spring, I keep an eye and ear out for the red-browed firetails. Their piercing 'see's' are almost inaudible, but when a dozen of them, who would fit onto the palms of my hands, decide to disport themselves in the birdbath, it is one of the best shows in Byron. When I hear the soft plashing of water and shaking of wings, I move stealthily. Slowly, I slink and glide out towards the deck where I have a ringside seat.

In the garden or the forest, there is always a possibility of surprise. One afternoon, the pair of pheasant coucals, who live in the forest, crash-landed in their rustle-and-crunch style in the spotted gum tree outside my bathroom where I was having a haircut. I was so excited to see them together and to view their barred plumage up so close, I nearly got my ear cut off when I jumped up to get a better view.

Just when I think I've accounted for all the new birds in my backyard, (I've identified thirty-four so far), a new one will turn up: an emerald dove, a scarlet honeyeater, a white-cheeked rosella, a buff-banded rail, a double-barred finch.

One autumn, when I was weeding around the young tree plantings in the forest, I heard a new voice. It was a spangled drongo, but it was up so high in a mature paperbark I couldn't get a good look at it. Okay, I said silently to the drongo. Your life is really none of my business. I'm snooping on you. I'll get off your territory now and if you want to show yourself to me some other time, you will.

Next morning, during breakfast, I heard rasping, hissing and cackling. There were six drongos dangling like shiny black fruits from the fronds of the banana tree and the fishtail palm. They tarried there for several minutes. Thanks fellas, I said. And off they flew.

Some days, I play the piano and sing. On an extra-energetic day, I might get stuck into the house cleaning, although the fanatical attention to detail with which I once approached, say, architrave-wiping, has faded with time. My house has the dust to prove it. Then there are the walks: on the beach, through the heath, to the lighthouse, in the rainforests, around the lake. If I examine the form and textures of my days and my desires, they bear almost no resemblance to those of the first half of my life. Proust said that the character a person developed in 'the latter half' of life was 'sometimes the exact reverse [of one's earlier characteristics], like a garment that has been turned'.

Also – and this is nothing new for me – I read. And read. And read. It bursts me out of my own small bubble and exposes me to a borderless world of aberrant characters, fantastic landscapes, extraordinary creatures and mind-thumping, if not -expanding, theories. Travel may broaden the mind, or these days, as life becomes increasingly homogenised, flatten it out. But reading can transport and completely remodel it.

In my readathons, I find out, for example:

• That more than a quarter of newly-paired gulls squabble and break up over who is going to sit on the eggs; that female fruit flies demand that their males be tender *and* macho. That the virtually brainless cockroach feels stress and humiliation and sometimes succumbs to suicide.

• That scientists estimate that a minimum of one hundred thousand planets like the Earth exist in our galaxy alone. Given that there are one hundred million galaxies (give or take) observable through our most powerful telescopes, this means that we can reckon on the existence of at least ten million planets 'more or less like our own'. So how special does that make us, after all?

• That the female emperor penguin passes her single egg to the male, who puts it on top of his feet and lowers a pouch of skin over the top. She then quits the colony to feed, returning when the egg is due to hatch. On her return, the male may not have fed for as long as three months and may have lost as much as forty-five per cent of his body weight. To reach the open sea, he then treks as far as 200 kilometres. 'If the female arrives after the egg has hatched, the male can feed the chick for up to two weeks with a milky secretion from his oesophagus.'

• That an infinite number of parallel universes may exist simultaneously and that matter (including human beings who may be 'exact duplicates of ourselves') exists in all of these as parallel ghosts.

Mother Nature interjects: In a parallel universe, your alter ego would have gone on a date with that smooth-talking physicist you met at Wilson's Creek – remember him? – but in this, your current physical reality, you did not.

• Australia, I discover, is the only continent which has not played host to the big cats. I learn that the Ugandan lions, increasingly marginalised by encroaching farmlands (and hunters with guns), have stopped roaring in an effort to save themselves. I consider my human need to communicate and how it would hurt to remain mute: that gives me a rough, agonising idea of what that enforced silence has cost the big felines and my throat closes over in compassion. And as for tigers, it is estimated that fewer than four thousand 'remain alive in the wild outside of the Sundarbans, where the world's last viable tiger population still clings. Most of the other tigers have been slaughtered by poachers and their bones have been ground up and sold as medicine in many Asian countries.' There will come a dark day when they will no longer burn bright, when their 'fearful symmetry' will be nothing more than a hollow, historic echo and frankly, I hope I'll be long gone when that time arrives.

Mother Nature says: In the cosmic overview, these species are choosing, on a very deep level, as humans do, the timing of their own departures from the physical plane, but that advanced understanding does not obviate your need to grieve the prospect of their passing and the loss of the richness they brought to life on your plane. You are living at a turning point in consciousness. During this time, all the kingdoms and queendoms of life, all species are facing serious survival problems and are re-evaluating the quality of life available to them. For the animals, like humans, may also deem life without meaning, or life filled with overwhelming suffering, or life which cripples the expansive challenge of their abilities, to be unviable. You humans need to re-embrace the natural world that birthed you, to rediscover the spirituality inherent in your biological origins and to become co-creative partners with the many species around you.

Along my meandering reading trail, I stumble across titles such as: *Creation Revisited: The Origin of Space, Time and the Universe*; *God and the New Physics*; *Wholeness and the Implicate Order*; *Cosmic Coincidences: Dark Matter, Mankind and Anthropic Cosmology*; *The Rebirth of Nature: The Greening of Science and God*; *The Mind of God: The Scientific Basis for a Rational World*; *God and the Astronomers*; *Quantum Cosmology and the Laws of Nature: Scientific Perspectives on Divine Action*.

What kind of cosmic cross-dressing is going on here? Is this just a case of publishers cashing in on current New Age trends? Or are these scientists (at last) really on to something? West is meeting East, left-brain is concurring with right-brain, rationalism is confirming mysticism. Let us hope, for the planet's sake, that the alpha and omega of this cosmic cohabitation is positive.

Geologian Thomas Berry claims science is 'a mythic form of understanding'. Since the advent of quantum physics, the more 'reflective scientists in a larger context are aware of the deeper mysteries of existence'. All scientific formulas, he believes, are 'as much myth and mystery' as they are 'rational understanding'. Formulas, without human under-standing, are useless, 'so the understanding is not in the formula'. Science does not diminish the mystery, he says, it enhances it.

Mother Nature writes: In all of these scientific endeav-ours, what is being proclaimed about the universe and your place and purpose within it is not a revo-lutionary cosmology (there is nothing new under the sun, only different ways of filtering the light) but a clear continuity of what the mystics, the seers, the shamans, the earth cultivators, artists and poets have always known. Your scientists are simply making physically real what the intuitive ones have always known: that there is a deeper reality underlying the three-dimensional physical one you perceive with your senses. This scientifically endorsed physicality will help those people who find it difficult to accept non-tangible truths to expand and deepen their perception. It is all part of the one great uplifting of consciousness on your plane.

Meanwhile, in this quiet chapter of my life, I happen to have the time to write down my learnings as they unfold. Weeks, months, seasons later, I dip into a book chosen at random and find the echoes, the gist of my own perceptions, sometimes exact adjectives, metaphors, staring uncannily up at me, from the pages.

Mother Nature files: If you wish to gasp over these simi-larities, that's up to you, my child. From my vantage point, I see only too clearly how your human lives, with their highly individual experiences and perceptions, still share deep commonalities across geographical space and through your linear time. As for your fretting over creative duplications, nature, in your physical reality, has always been a touchstone of contemplation, wisdom and inspiration for humankind, so there are bound to be repetitions. You cannot copyright the collective unconscious. Since time is actually open-ended, existing in multiple, simultaneous presents, who's to say who thought what first? These ideas are sitting out there in the cosmos just waiting for someone to log on, download and print them out. Better get on with it, then.

Through the growth and decay of several seasons, I lounged on the deck and faded into some remarkable worlds. I met the redoubtable Ellis Rowan (1848-1922) an Australian artist whose work won international respect during her lifetime, but has since slipped into obscurity. Using her poor health and artistic inclination as excuses (it seems to me) to escape from Melbourne winters, motherhood and a bad marriage to a patriarchal military man, Ellis travelled to some of the most rugged landscape of Australia, New Zealand, New Guinea and, later, the USA. She was one of the great, intrepid Victorian artistic explorers. In fifty years, she painted three thousand pictures of flowers, insects and birds. Ellis viewed her art as a tribute to nature. Venturing into the broiling depths of the New Guinea rainforest, she managed to paint forty-five of the fifty-two known species of birds of paradise. An image of her in an immaculate, long constricting gown, high-button boots, paintbrush in one hand, a writhing bird of paradise under the other arm, stays with me yet. As do her exacting paintings of those brilliant birds.

I said to her: Ellis, no wonder you did the flit on that rigid, controlling husband. Military intelligence endures as one of the great oxymorons.

Late at night, by lamplight, I met Marie Curie, who isolated the highly radioactive substance of radium which later was used to treat growths, tumours and certain kinds of cancer. From 1898 to 1902, she and her husband Pierre toiled in gruelling conditions in a lumber room and an abandoned shed in Paris. Marie took on the 'man's job'. She later wrote, 'I sometimes passed the whole day stirring a boiling mass (of pitch-blende) with an iron rod nearly as big as myself. In the evening, I was broken with fatigue.' Her daughter Eve later wrote: 'In the courtyard, dressed in her old dust-covered and acid-stained smock, her hair blown by the wind, surrounded by smoke which stung her eyes and throat, Marie was a sort of factory all by herself.' When Marie finally managed to prepare a decigram of pure radium, the disbelieving chemists, according to Eve, 'could only bow before the facts, before the superhuman obstinacy of a woman. Radium officially existed.'

I said to her: Madame (for I could not bring myself to address her as Marie), during those difficult years when you were shovelling and stirring and purifying, I find it remarkable that you never gave up hope, although your husband asked you to desist, although you had a four-year-old daughter to care for and Pierre was often jealous of your attentions to the child. All I can say is: Viva La Femme!

One afternoon while walking the beach, I ran into a writer friend. He insisted that *Sexual Personae* was a must-read. I gave myself a 700-page-plus earful of Camille Paglia's views on Western life, art, thought, sex and nature. Paglia's discourse is, by her own admission, 'a form of sensationalism'. She sees nature and sex as 'brutal pagan forces'. She warned that: 'Every time we say nature is beautiful, we are saying a prayer, fingering our worry beads.' And that 'nature has a master agenda we can only dimly know.' 'Let nature shrug,' she finger-wagged, 'and all is in ruin.'

I said to her: Ms Paglia, there *is* another view, a radical one which holds that we are not at the mercy of so-called natural catastrophes, but rather the creators of them.

And I proceeded to quote Seth, my favourite 'energy personality essence'[1]:

'You divorce yourself from nature and nature's intents far more than the animals do. Nature in its stormy manifestations seems like an adversary. You must either look for reasons outside of yourselves to explain what seems to be nature's ill intent at such times, or its utter lack of concern.

'Science often says that nature cares little for the individual, only for the species, so then you must see yourselves as victims in a larger struggle for survival, in which your own intents do not carry even the puniest sway ...

'Your planet has a body as much as you have. Your blood follows certain prescribed patterns and so does the wind. You are *inside* the <u>body</u> of the earth in those terms. As cells within your body influence it, so does your *body* affect the larger body of the earth. The weather faithfully reflects the feelings of the individuals in any given local territory. Overall weather patterns follow deeper inner rhythms of emotion.

'Those in earthquake regions are attracted to such spots because of their innate understanding of the astonishing relationship between exterior circumstances and their own quite private mental and emotional patterns.'

Hear, hear!

It was Mother Nature, eavesdropping. Who could blame Her? A moot question – in more ways than one.

Over many light snacks and cups of tea, I met Emily Dickinson, a lawyer's daughter from Amherst, Massachusetts (1830-86). She was a vivacious person, but she progressively withdrew into an almost totally reclusive existence 'by deliberate and conscious choice'. Dickinson, the critics seem to agree, is one of the greatest lyric poets of all time. During her own lifetime, she was an undiscovered genius. Only seven of her 1775 poems were published before her death. She had immense vision and passionate intensity and awe of life, love, nature, time and eternity.

She wrote to her literary mentor, Thomas Higginson: 'To live is so startling, it leaves but little room for other occupations.' An American expert said: 'All pity for Miss Dickinson's "starved life" is misdirected. Her life was one of the richest and deepest ever lived on the continent.' Critics searching for 'sources in her external life to account for the rich and vivid life of the poems' find themselves dead-ended at every turn. One writer pointed out that Emily 'led, quite consciously, a metaphorical life'.

Dickinson's 'cynical surrealism' was, according to Paglia, unmatched among great women writers. Here is a short Dickinson take on the spiritual: 'God was penurious with me, which makes me shrewd with Him.' Or what about this quick chop at nature: 'Split the lark and you'll find the music.'

I said to her: Emily, perhaps you should have gone out more. But then, so perhaps, should I.

* * *

So there I was, holed up with all these wonderful kin who jumped off the pages and kept me up late and got me up early, telling me all about themselves.

These confabulations continued on my beach walks. I would round up a few companionable suspects – characters or creatures – from this ethereal coterie. Never mind that they were alive or dead, near or far 'in the usual terms'. If I felt deflated or anxious as I strode along, I would revisit their trials, their triumphs, their passion for living. I would gaze up, down and all around me at nature's anodyne paraphenalia, and my spirits would soon begin to rise.

This is quite a world we've got here, I'd enthuse to the air, the parallel universes, the whole shebang.

And in my ear Mother Nature would trumpet: And thus it ever was and ever more shall be.

1. Beginning in late 1963, Jane Roberts, from her home in New York State, channelled numerous books for Seth. Her husband Robert F. Butts took notes as she spoke in trance. She died in 1984.

____

19

Clear Sailing and Shipwreck

As the days went by, I discovered so many fascinating new aspects of nature, so many marvels and mysteries, that I worried I would run out of time to explore and synthesise them into my writing before I was dragged – kicking, screaming and up to my red-rimmed eyeballs in hock – back into more worldly pursuits.

Conditioned by years of urgent, imminent writing deadlines, I whipped myself up into a wave of panic and began to focus intently on the finishing line. Some days, snagged in the thick undergrowth of the work, I found it, frankly, hard going. Dear Reader, I hope this next admission won't put you off. But in those prickly patches, doing the daily writing was like pulling teeth. Like draining blood from a stone. Lonely. A slog.

One week during this phase I read *The Moor's Last Sigh* by Salman Rushdie (now there's someone who's grappled with creating in isolation[1]) and he made me feel worse. I envied his picaresque rendering of Indian life in all its spicy bizarreness; upon myself I wished his wit and rollercoaster wordplay. I particularly enjoyed this paragraph for its pertinence to life in the Bay:

'Have you noticed that Benengeli is defined by what it lacks – that unlike much of the region, certainly unlike the whole Costa, it is devoid of such excrescences as Coco-Loco nightclubs, coach parties on guided tours, burro-taxis, currency cambios, and vendors of straw sombreros. Our excellent Sargento, Salvador Medina, drives all such horrors away by administering nocturnal beatings, in the village's many dark alleys, to any entrepreneur who seeks to introduce them. Salvador Medina dislikes me intensely, by the way, as he dislikes all the town's newcomers, but like all well-settled immigrants – like the great majority of the Parasites – I applaud his policy of repulsing the new wave of invaders. Now that we're in, it's only right that somebody should slam the door shut behind us.'

To my knowledge, we don't have a Sargento Medina at the local cop shop, but should one ever rock up, I reckon he should run for mayor. So you see, Rushdie made me laugh and that was a real treat at a time when laughter was approaching endangered species status with me. I didn't care much for Rushdie's characters, but that was a tiny grain of grit in the eye as I was swept along by the monsoonal carpet ride of his style. And what's more, his text read as if it had all just tumbled effortlessly out of his brain one fine morning over his chapatis and chai, as if it could hardly squeeze itself between the colorful covers and threatened to spill to a second fat volume.

I grew arbitrary about when I thought my manuscript *should be finished*. Every few hours during the writing, I would call up the spellcheck and review the wordcount. It never seemed to be enough. What a tangled web I'd started to weave on account of mixing it with that Mother Nature. Like an insect caught deep inside a Venus flytrap, I was starting to wonder

if I would ever get out. But I doggedly kept on at the work,
until one day a little memo came through from Mother Nature:

———————————

My Dear Child,

I see that your writing is gradually toughening into
an armour of hasty achievement, duty and embattled
persistence. This approach will not serve you nor
enhance the quality and value of the work.

I ask you: does a peach hurry unduly to ripen on
the bough? Generally, I'm not one for Bible quota-
tions, but this one seems particularly apt: 'Consider
the lilies of the field, how they grow: they toil not,
neither do they spin.'

Firstly, I want to assure you there is plenty of time
for everything you need to say and do in this lifetime.
Everything comes to fruition in its own perfect, if
unpredictable timing. There is no need to rush or
force things prematurely.

Secondly, comparing yourself in any respect with
others is as pointless as comparing apples with
oranges. Each being is stamped with a unique blueprint of purpose, personality, personal talents and
predilections. You must trust your own abilities and
follow your own stars of invention, no matter how
faintly they sometimes shine.

Thirdly, when it comes to your creativity, ask yourself what it is you love most, what you most believe in,
feel inspired by, and celebrate those sentiments for as

long as they hold true for you. This attitude will help to lift you out of the mental miasma you've gotten yourself into.

You need to focus on and *enjoy* the material to hand, the expansion and creativity latent in each moment.

Love, etcetera,

M.N.

I did my best to assimilate this advice as I proceeded with the writing. I lightened up, I kept on walking the land and allowing it to move me, I stopped comparing myself; I tried to stay in the moment as much as possible. Instead of scheming where and how to include everything I was absorbing about nature, I relaxed and savoured each morsel of discovery. I stopped checking the wordcount and wrote with my focus on each sentence as it unfolded.

As a result, something in me energetically shifted until one day I felt I had reached a point of creative critical mass – and from this point there erupted a chain reaction which, once in full swing, I scarcely knew how to curb.

My library card grew so activated it almost blipped itself across the counter. The vapour trails had transmogrified into a network of clear pathways covering the planet's uncountable yesterdays, todays and tomorrows.

Once I was on the road, so to speak, I got so hot on the scent of these nature trails they began to show up in my dreams. I would find myself submerged in the bottom of the sea, ablaze in the torrid centre of the Earth or pouring milk onto it from my breasts[2], drifting in the dark void of space, ascending as a giant kingfisher[3] above a wasteland and descending into yet another green garden. All the trails – outside on the landscape and inside on the dreamscape –

seemed to crisscross one another in endless intersections. Linear time lost its meaning as past, present and future converged during my esoteric expeditions to places as disparate as Walden Pond[4], Bingen[5], Tinker Creek[6] and Bollingen[7]. The mysterious creative seams of the unconscious began to rise up and burst through the volatile crust of my waking life, flowing like tongues of lava down the slippery slopes of my solitude, blanketing themselves over the most mundane and commonplace matters. I never knew where they would lead me next. All I knew was that paramnesia or not[8], I was bound to follow.

Mother Nature: The boundaries between your inner and outer worlds are illusory; it is only your perception (acquired from the mental constructs of your society) which separates them. Some of you have experienced this sense of boundlessness when you allow your ego-self to drop away and your deeper self to merge with nature or with another being during transcendent lovemaking; others have felt it during your meditations or dreams. When you express your creativity, you automatically begin to link your waking and dreaming selves. The two synthesise into new mental models which are equally at home in either of those realities.

As for 'time,' your Aboriginal peoples have always understood there is no schism between time and eternity. They recognise the totemic, visible landscape as an essential and intact part of what is, for them, the unquestioned reality of eternity.

The irresistible compulsion with which, in recent times, I had assiduously removed myself from the outer world, gradually began to make additional sense in a creative context. So this was why George Bernard Shaw 'left family, friends, business and Ireland' and spent roughly 'eight years in absentia, writing constantly'; it was why Australian novelist David Malouf hung out in Tuscany for so many years; why the late artist Ian Fairweather lived for decades like a hermit in a shack on Bribie Island; why artist Lawrence Daws resides in a secluded Queensland paradise near the Glasshouse Mountains. While I did not presume to rank myself in the same creative class as these folk, I bet myself they could all tell me a thing or two about retreat and about art as invocation.

It's hard to explain to non-writers, let alone non-readers, how you can get so wrapped up in the eros of language. In this geyser phase of the writing, I found myself in love not only with the creative process, but with the lexicon, enamoured by the idea of language as gesture, in awe of it as a rite of gratitude, fascinated by how its phonetics and etymology often express 'the wisdom of the unconscious'.

Don de Lillo talks about the 'isolated pleasure, the lonely, deep, intimate and unspoken satisfaction [a writer] takes in putting words together. To open up the sentence, to loosen the screws of punctuation and syntax.' Late at night, notebook in my lap, I would lie in the lilied arms of language; I would play with diction, feeling the words rise up, tasting their sweet and sour insinuations, taking my time to reach a contented conclusion. Sometimes I would please myself with poetry, whispering the words or calling them out loud, letting them caress my ears with their soft and tender consonants, contract my throat with their plosive glottal stops, bruise my lips with their hurried, craving intent, their irresistible 'color of saying'. And always, I remained mindful of Emily's warning: 'We must be careful what we say. No bird resumes its egg.'

Happy as a sand crab in my seaside hidey-hole, I was on a roll, and the further I allowed myself to be carried into my right mind, the more the subterranean channels opened, the more the dictated disclosures flowed through, and the harder it became to attend to the essential mundanities of life. I skipped meals, skolled protein supplement drinks, left the answer machine on and grew tardy about returning calls. For the first time in my adult life, I left my bed unmade – every day. Miss Hospital Corners was relegated to a tiny back room in my psyche. To leave the computer to water the garden or do the washing was a wrench. Going 'out' to buy the groceries degenerated into a distracting chore I resented and postponed until there was not a grain of rice or a shred of toilet paper in the house. In that concentrated phase, I understood why it was that men, singularly focussed on their own personal goals, often wished so keenly to secure for themselves a wife. I wished I had one myself.

Although I missed the fresh sugar-cane-and-ginger juice and the cheap potted plants, I also gave a miss to the local markets, those casbahs of casual social encounters; and I rationed the mail box collection from daily to weekly. After all, I was not expecting any cheques, and the post office in this town is a cornerstone of even closer collisions of the chatty kind. Inside my bell-jar of imagination and focus, I didn't want anyone to disturb me, to tip me upside down and cover my clear inner landscape with the snowy confetti of their conversation – their tree planting, their new nightshade-free diet, their feral teenagers (second only to wallabies as a threat to thriving marijuana crops), their conspiracy theories, their gripes about the Shire Council.

During those astral weeks, I was simultaneously wired and exhausted, for Mother Nature had taken to waking me several times throughout the night, sometimes for as little as a word, sometimes for as much as several pages:

'Wake up and write this down!' she would press and importune. And I would switch on the bedside lamp and, sleepy-eyed, scribble obligingly on the paper.

Next day, like a mid-life nursing mother, I would be ragged with the tiredness of broken sleep, but I could not rest much during the day either because the demands of this new creation, this hungry, growing baby of a book kept tugging on me. Pardon my mixing up my goddesses and my metaphors here, but I puzzled: how had Gaia managed to pour out all that milk and not have 'custom stale Her infinite variety'?[9] On those bone-weary days I felt nothing like Gaia and, if truth be told, I looked very little like Cleopatra and very much like the Creature from the Black Lagoon.

In the library one day, I was trying to find out more about the spectacular Morning Glory roll cloud, a phenomenon which occurs near Normanton and Burketown on the western side of Cape York and only during October. The cloud rolls in at dawn and can be hundreds of kilometres in length, travelling up to eighty kilometres[10] per hour. A young man typing on one of the computers overheard my request to the staff and offered to put me in touch with his uncle who was, he said, a meteorologist. Then I sought some details about strangler figs like the one I'd seen in Wanganui. The woman standing beside me at the counter spoke up and offered two local contacts; both people, she assured me, would be able to tell me everything I had ever yearned to know about strangler figs but had been afraid to ask. What was going on here? This must be how a bar magnet feels when, from out of the blue, heaps of iron filings suddenly fly in thick and fast and stick to it. This must be what happens for the satin bower bird when he sets his intent to attract a mate and begins to scavenge for trinkets with which to make splendid his nest.

Feeling chipper, I left the library and set off up the street. Next thing Mother Nature launched into the singing telegram:

'When it's not always raining there'll be days like this
When there's no one complaining there'll be days like this
When everything falls into place like the flick of a switch
Well my mama told me there'll be days like this.'

Did you write that?

No. Van Morrison did. But I thought you might like to hear it, since you're having such a good day. Now seriously, about this business of the puzzle pieces coming together. Let me tell you what the alchemists understood about this. They stated that whenever you delineate the space for which you are responsible, whatever you need will be brought to you within that space. The whole cosmos will conspire in your favour, raining down onto you its lucky dip of treasures, its colorful flotsam and jetsam, its white wisps of light to be used for its – and your – higher purpose. For the two purposes run parallel. To attract that influx, however, first you need to align with your higher purpose. Begin by demonstrating your trust in its fulfilment. To make this demonstration, you'll need to muster the courage to make a start on whatever it is you want to achieve. Do what you can each day – no matter how slight or seemingly inconsequential – and trust that for every step you take towards achieving your goals, the Divine will take several towards you.

The pace of the writing escalated until I felt I was being hurtled through a creative flash flood, trying to keep my voice-filled head above the rushing runnel, attempting to note things down before this powerful gusher dumped me like a dab of debris, then receded, leaving me high, dry, and stranded, as I feared it must. Swept up in this momentum, I abandoned the civilised and sensible Bloomsbury school of writing I had been following for months on this manuscript – at the desk from nine to twelve-thirty, lunch, then leisurely afternoon pursuits – walking, reading, gardening, napping. Instead, I began to spend seven, eight, nine barely interrupted hours at a time at the keyboard – six, sometimes seven days a week, for weeks. During that febrile phase I trebled the length of the manu-script, but inevitably even The Muse bowed to the pressure of physical fatigue. Something, somewhere, had to give ...

One morning I woke up and realised that the inspirational flash flood had indeed receded, leaving in its wake a pile of handwritten notes and annotations waiting to be typed and a waterfall of pain inside my left arm which dangled, inert, swollen and aching with tendonitis. The physically inevitable had occurred. RSI, that dreaded wraith of creative sabotage, had reared up and almost wrecked the whole gig. Robert Graves was spot-on when he wrote:

'The Muse alone is licensed to do murder
And to betray: weeping with honest tears
She thrones each victim in her paradise.'

Equally accurate was the doctor who explained, 'RSI is not

an injury at all ... It's the body's best attempt to handle a circumstance it doesn't like. When a muscle stays contracted for an extended period, like arm muscles do when we type, toxins accumulate and the muscles can go into spasm. Over time, that muscle will adapt to its demands by becoming more like ligaments and bones – those tissues that are designed to bear static loads.'

I stopped typing. Immediately. My salad days of writing, were, at least for some time, over. What to do? Well, nothing much, for a whole healing season, the early part of which found me frustrated and low-spirited. Still deeply self-defined by doing and strongly identified with physical vitality, I was required once again to question my identity and my value in a life stripped of creative accomplishment and energetic activity as I'd come to know and depend on them.

In due course, Mother Nature, like a benevolent bedouin bearing the fresh water of the (last) Word, arrived and spoke. I tape-recorded her message.

My Dear Child,

I see you are preoccupied with your arm, with your finances, with your uncertain future. May I suggest that you take your fearful focus off those things and give some attention to your feet.

My feet?!

Yes, your feet. If you want to understand your

relationship to the Earth; if you want to stay balanced and grounded – connected to the earth as a conductor of dynamic vitality – in everything you think and communicate and do; if you wish to intuit your destiny, you need to move those feet. If you use only your head, as you have been doing lately, you will stay stuck in your intellect. Go outdoors, walk and dance again on the earth. Ground yourself, rest yourself, heal yourself, recover your own balanced rhythm of doing and being, working and playing, dreaming and creating, thinking and feeling.

The journey into the Feminine is about being and becoming, not goal-setting and achieving. The Feminine is not compelled to heroically pit its will against adversity as a form of self-identification. Rather, it lives and identifies itself in the present, in the stream of countless moments that constitute your existence. Things can change radically in a moment. One moment you breathe in, next moment you breathe out. If you do more of one than the other, your physical life will tip out of balance and, in extremis, snuff out. For months now, you have been breathing *out out* in your creative writing flow. Now your body is telling you it is time to pause again, to take a big, deep breath in.

Some moments, some days, sailing through unchartered passages of life, you will drift closer to the shore. You'll feel as if you're starting to getting it all together, as if you're in a sheltered cove and about to be washed up onto some some wilder shore of love or opportunity. Other days you will be cast adrift in the vast ocean of life, with no sign of a shoreline or even a horizon, no passing ships and, during the darkest nights of the soul, not even the reassuring or guiding twinkle of a single star. Some days you may suffer, as you did just experience with your writing, a shipwreck, a sudden reversal when you least expect or want it. Since the fates of your own unconscious, unresolved personal issues are always rolling the dice, this result of wrong attitude usually turns out to be just the number you need in that moment, for it provides the opportunity for you to plumb your true depths.

And if perchance, you wash up on a desert island for a while, that, too, is a good opportunity to reassess things – like your behavioural extremes, your motives, your beliefs – is it not? Stranded on that island, you may feel afraid, lost, utterly alone. You may ask: why did this have to happen to me? Or: why does this always happen to me? It never seems to happen to others. Or: other people always seem to have it easier. Dear child, from where I'm sitting, monitoring with my all-seeing eye the complicated shipping news of the world, let me assure you that you are not Robinson Crusoe. There are hairline fractures and deep fissures beneath the splendidly painted hulls of each being's persona. Every person suffers shipwreck – over and over again in many different facets of his or her life. And each shipwreck provides an opportunity to dive in search of those gold doubloons, those deeper truths about yourselves and your place in the world. I invite you to redefine 'suffering'. Try perceiving it not as something to be bypassed at all costs and at all times, but as the painful exertion inherent in any growth process.

Take responsibility for your shipwreck, yes. But do not give yourself fifty lashes over it, for shipwreck is an inevitable and invaluable part of learning. It is just energy moving through you and changing things. Insane though this proposition initially may sound, try to embrace it. It is *life*!

Those stranded interludes can begin to change or in some instances, can completely change, as I mentioned, in an instant. Ask for help and I promise you that someone or something will show up to help you, to bring you sustenance, to give you shelter, to help you to repair the damage, to help you to heal your sorrows and uncertainties, to assist you to replot your course, to rebuild your vessel and voyage onwards. Eventually you will sight land ahoy. Patience and trust. Patience and trust. There is so much help available from the hidden realities, yet so few of you call out for it – and so infrequently. You struggle along inside that 'sealed' bubble of physical reality and forget to connect with the subtle realms, with The Invisibles. There are legions of helpers and guides – a scene too numerous to tell – waiting to be of service to you if you would only ask. Remember: ask and it shall be given. Not always in the form you want, but always in the mode you most need.

With love and light,

Mother Nature.

The unconditionality of that reiterated promise struck some deep chord of gratitude in me and I began to weep. There was no use looking for a tissue. I never bought them on account of the trees. Paper towels were out for the same reason. I tried the loo for toilet paper. No joy there. I tried the kitchen for a tea towel. All the tea towels were stashed in the overflowing laundry basket, awaiting a wash. Desperate, I tried my wardrobe for a handkerchief. No luck there, either. As a last resort, I grabbed a pair of pink cotton knickers. I sat on the bedroom floor and had a good cry. When the emotion had subsided, I thought: How embarrassing to cry over your own copy! Better not admit that to anyone. They'd think I'd really gone troppo.

In the bathroom as I washed my face, I thought: there's something familiar about that crying-over-your-own-copy business.

In that moment, however, memory failed to retrieve it.

It will come to me, I prompted, as I patted my eyes dry with a soft towel.

When in doubt, have a cup of tea. I drank it on the deck and looked at the garden. After a solid rainy season, the plants had grown prolifically, especially the parrot's beak heliconias[11], which, for some reason, always cheered me.

Pssst!

It was You Know Who:

That plant is aptly named. Helicon, a mountain in Greece, in Boeotia is the location of the springs of Hippocrene and Aganippe, believed by the ancient Greeks to be the sacred source of poetic inspiration and the house of the Muses. So in today's language, 'heliconian' still means inspirational or uplifting. You see, I told you there is a reason for everything. I will send to you a carrier pigeon from the heliconias.

146

What did She mean, a carrier pigeon? She could be cryptic sometimes. Oh well, I would just have to wait.

My back garden was starting to look decidedly jungley. Suddenly, an image of Kathleen Turner in the South American jungle popped into mind; then my internal eye swivelled to replay the opening scene of *Romancing the Stone*. In that scene, Kathleen's character had cried over her typewriter as she finished writing the final pages – the happy ending – of her latest romance novel. What escapades she had embarked on in that film! Her peaceful existence as an authoress was turned upside down when she received a map in the mail from her soon-to-be-murdered brother-in-law and then a frantic plea for help from her sister. Almost before she knew it she found herself in the middle of a gun battle in the Columbian jungle. Teaming up with Michael Douglas, who played a bird trader and all-out adventurer, she found herself up to her unlaced bodice in high jinks, temptation and fast-moving drama. He, of course, eventually followed her to New York and in the final scene the pair kissed on the deck of his brand new yacht as the music surged and the credits rolled. Natch. Hollywood dares not disappoint nor digress from its standard platitudes, its predictable formulae, its conventional endings with all suffering redeemed, all rectitude rewarded, all stray ends tied up.

My sister and brother-in-law, when last heard from, were both alive and well and doing business as usual in the Sydney rock music jungle. So much for my chances of the Columbian episode. (And besides, I do like my brother-in-law.)

As a postscript, I seemed to recall that Turner's character had even dredged another best-selling novel out of her romance with the bird trader. I chortled.

Impulsively I decided to consult Emily on this matter.

I said to her: Emily, perhaps we should have written bodice rippers ... But then again, perhaps not.

Emily, never one for a long girls' rave, replied succinctly:

'The soul selects her own society.'

She might have added another acute sentence or two had she not been overtaken in the etheric intervention stakes by Mother Nature.

My dear Emily, you are indeed on the right track here. If you would forgive my interruption ...

————————

My Dear Child,

If you would be willing – and I see that you are willing – to hear me out, I have a few ideas to share with you. In your Western society, I notice, your arthouse movies and 'literary' novels often promote the depressing notion of human powerlessness, of woman, say, as the victim of her social environment. Your highly educated or intellectual types criticise from a great height the stereotyping and predictability of cultural products such as this *Romancing the Stone*. And yet dramas such as these demonstrate your human ability to venture forward, to take action and to achieve a longed-for outcome, to manifest your heart's desire. When you patronisingly label these productions as adult fairy tales, you crush the child in you who once instinctively knew that, through wishing, it is simpler to bring into being happy outcomes than sad ones.

And although life's letdowns can make it difficult for you to believe again in this mental mastery, I encourage you to remind yourself that dreams come true through your own intimate intent, design and behaviour, and not, as it superficially appears, by chance. Remember: what you focus on grows; your thoughts and beliefs are the seeds from which grow the shape and sway of all your days.

With love and light,

Mother Nature.

1. After the publication of Rushdie's novel *The Satanic Verses* in 1988, the Ayotollah Khomeni issued a fatwa calling for the author's execution. Rushdie was forced into hiding, changing locations frequently.
2. It is said that a mythic Gaia poured milk from her breasts and they became galaxies.
3. Edward C. Whitmont in *Return of the Goddess* (Page 170) writes: 'the Waste Land, and the injury to male creativity (the wound of the Fisher King) are owing to the disregard of the great Feminine. Restoration of land and man depends on restoring homage to her.' See recommended reading.
4. Walden Pond was the home of American essayist/naturalist Henry David Thoreau. See footnote at end of Chapter 14.
5. Hildegard of Bingen was a twelfth century German abbess, poet, composer and 'grandmother of the Rhineland mystics', extraordinarily ecological in her worldview.
6. Annie Dillard won the 1975 Pulitzer Prize for *Pilgrim at Tinker Creek*, 'a rich and colorful chronicle of the changing seasons at Tinker Creek, a valley in the Blue Ridge Mountains of Virginia.'
7. Bollingen, situated by the scenic upper lake of Zurich, is where in 1922 Swiss psychologist Carl Gustav Jung bought some land and built 'a suitable dwelling tower' in which 'the feeling of repose and renewal' he had 'was intense from the start'.
8. A disorder of the memory or the faculty of recognition in which dreams may be confused with reality.
9. 'Age cannot wither her, nor custom stale her infinite variety.' Enobarbus in Shakespeare's *Antony and Cleopatra*.
10. The only other known appearance of a roll cloud is in the Gulf of Mexico once a year.
11. *Heliconia rostrata*. An upright clumping, tropical plant 1.5-2.5 metres tall with banana-like foliage, bright red, yellow and green pendulous flowers in late spring/summer. Exquisite.

20

The Blessing of Beauty

Near where I live is a ti-tree lake, known in local Aboriginal lore as the women's lake. It is believed that before white settlement the lake was frequented by the Indigenous women, the Arakwal clan of the Bunjalung nation. In particular, it's said that the pregnant women bathed in it because of the therapeutic properties of the ti-tree oil.

An unspoiled place, it's surrounded by bush, steeped in tranquillity, and one white-winged morning in mid-winter I set off, via the beach, to spend some time there. En route I hoped to spot whales, for the humpbacks were on their annual migratory path from the Antarctic to the tropical waters off the Queensland coast to breed. I was in luck. A mother and calf coasted just beyond the breakers, blowing spume and tail fluking. Seeing this play gladdened me, although it was neither my first nor my closest sighting of those lurching leviathans. My friends Trish and Wally Franklin, who have spent as much time in close contact with humpbacks as any researchers on the planet, say that such glimpses satisfy 'important human needs' which cannot be quantified in economic or political terms. The inner growth resulting from such encounters does not show up in the gross national product, or in the sterile bottom line of the economic rationalists.

In the 1950s, Byron Bay was one of Australia's major whaling stations. By 1959 the Byron Bay Whaling Company was granted a quota of one hundred and fifty whales (who in those times averaged ten tons). But by 1960, the whalers had almost wiped out the humpbacks and the barbaric practice was finished. Attitudes, thankfully, have changed and these days the only whales being shot around here are those sighted through the telescopic camera lenses of the whale-watching tourists who cluster around the Cape during the migration season.

When the whales had swum out of sight, I dawdled a while near a colony of crested terns in case a couple of them decided to turn on one of their spectacular paired mating flights. But they were all occupied with what appeared to be their morning ablutions and grooming. A southerly buster ruffled their shaggy black caps so they resembled a bunch of preening teenagers with mohawk haircuts.

I turned inland, following a shallow amber thread of water back to its source. The lake's broad waters were placid and turbid as dark treacle, the perfect inscrutable consort for the faded sky which was dimpled by a white half-moon in the west. The tracks lacing the sandy shore cut through dense scrubby vegetation, a chaotic genius of canopy, understorey and groundcover – wallum banksias, broadleafed paperbarks, ti-trees, swamp- and black she oaks proliferated, sheltering grass trees (fetching small fortunes in city nurseries these days), eggs and bacon bushes, lilies, irises, twining snake vines and the tiny ground-hugging and carnivorous sun dews plant which eats ants for breakfast.

Like so much of the Australian bush with its muted, grey-green and brown tones, this was not a place that socked you in the eye with a gaudy or grand beauty. But, alive with the croaky calls of wattle birds, the startling flashes of yellow on honeyeaters mid-flight, the thin notes of red-backed fairy wrens in the undergrowth, the murmurations of a zephyr through the tall, dry reeds and rushes, the bush radiated its own vibrant appeal.

That morning it was not a panorama I wanted (although the human eye naturally sees in panorama, in sweeps of roughly one hundred and forty degrees), but the intimacy of a sunny nook, so I retraced my steps to the seaward neck of the lake and, loose-limbed, all eyes, all ears, nestled against a grassy bank. A welcome swallow flitted back and forth across the water, deftly skimming within inches of its surface. To my ears, its song was a long quiet, rambling twitter, but another bird would have heard the swallow's song as a much more complicated rendition. Such birdsongs often feature a detailed pattern of melody and rhythm, but they are broadcast so fast that humans can only identify them as a twittering, like a tape of our speech on fast forward. Although we hear sounds over a similar range to birds, they can hear ten times faster than us. Who then lives in the richer world, stereophonically speaking?

From the upper branches of a casuarina tree, a brahminy kite lifted off, performing a series of slow, fluid arabesques over the channel before cruising north on its solitary hunting rounds. On the opposite bank, the shallow water's slight ripples were mirrored as silver ribbons of wavy light on the pale, flaky trunks of paperbark trees. With a softened gaze, I watched those light waves. Time passed. I closed my eyes to help the entrenched, eagle-eyed observer in me, the one who always has to apprehend, to gradually let go. I allowed my shoulders to drop and my mind to be carried along as if by the water's current. An image of my heliconias came to me, bringing to light a dream from the previous evening. In that dream, the heliconias had 'spoken' to me.

'See how we're always sending up new shoots? We let them all come up to the surface, to grow tall and stand together in a supportive clump. That's why we're beautiful.'

So this was the promised carrier pigeon. She knows a thing or two, that Mother Nature.

I sat very still, breathing and listening, until the flickering light behind my eyelids faded out, until the place's serenity began to permeate me, until she and I grew seamless.

* * *

That evening, in my garden, I sat on a rock and arranged around me a semi-circle of citronella candles. Under a fine spread of stars, I inhaled the candles' lemon scent and exhaled my thanks for all the beauty I'd encountered and absorbed in my time on this plane. Beauty, I realised, had informed and directed large tracts of my life, much as the stars have always done for mariners and for certain migratory breeds of birds.

Since childhood, my perception of beauty had been principally and inextricably linked to nature. Like a döppleganger sparking the embers of cherished memory, it lingered, even decades after the original physical formation had been obliterated by a dam, a freeway or a new housing development. In quest of beauty, I had variously moved house, borrowed money (to renovate), fallen in love, created a garden, travelled afield.

Yet as I pondered, a 'modern', dissenting voice inside my

head spoke up, playing devil's advocate, denigrating beauty and giving it a bad rap. 'Beauty is in the eye of the beholder,' it said, trotting out a tired and cynical cliche. I countered with Matthew Fox's claim that this facile and glib dismissal of beauty occurs because 'harmony and cosmos are so little dealt with. Beauty alerts us to our cosmic connections.' A dyed-in-the rainforest Romantic, I threw in some classic Keats, too:' ''Beauty is truth, truth beauty,'' – that is all Ye know on earth, and all ye need to know.' And a succinct swipe of Blake: 'Everything that lives is Holy.'

The dissenting voice grew a little shrill in its demands for me to recant: You Romantics live in a dream world, eschewing science and the hard, dark facts of life, it said. So I parried with a few insights from Peter Marshall's *Nature's Web*: 'Romanticism not only offers a modern way of experiencing reality, but forms the basis of a truly ecological sensibility.' For Romantics see the universe as a living organism, an organic whole. Through their exuberant pursuit of individual expression, they, like most ecologists, esteem unity in diversity. They have a love of unspoiled natural environments, of wilderness and pristine places. They intuit the divine presence in all things and in their desire to interpret nature, are avid explorers of all levels of consciousness.

What a tragedy of our times that beauty needs to be sanctioned, I thought. Fox claims that Westerners lost beauty when we lost the creation-centred spiritual traditions – in effect, when we lost the cosmos.

And so the dialectics went, until, weary of them, I dropped into meditation ... Afterwards, the candles were burning low. It was late and I wanted to sleep, for at first light I was going to the Belongil estuary to bird-watch.

My Dear Child,

Never give up your prizing and celebrating of
beauty, for it is a positive force more powerful, more
enduring, more restorative and healing than all the
rhetoric and polemic on your planet.

Beauty bestows hope and inspiration. Beauty
beckons the mystic and the artist in every person.
Beauty points the way to perceiving other planes.
Beauty has the capacity to expand you, to release you
from the jail-cell of your identity and transport you
to heightened and ecstatic realities. Beauty triggers
in you gratitude and awe. These are expansive energies; the more you experience and express them, the
more you are able to draw to you the essence of their
source. So beauty can set you on that upward spiral
of attraction and manifestation.

Beauty is not the exclusive province of that elite
band of professional artists you read about in your
textbooks and Saturday newspapers, just as heaven
does not belong to the vast empty cosmic space of the
scientists. Both live within your reach; both emanate
and move within and around your being.

Beauty extends beyond the visible and the
tangible, and dwells also in the non-material realms,
in the unbounded territory of your soul. Every
person, child or adult, young or old, is an instrument
of beauty – not only in the talents you possess, in the

work you may do, but also through the way you create your life, the way you relate to all sentient beings. Beauty resonates in the heart as much as it flickers before the eyes.

Like an amaranth, that imaginary flower that never fades, beauty is a pure, loving energy that lives eternally within you. This is one of my greatest gifts to you and its expression is one of your main purposes in this life. In this way you may return a gift to the very cosmos that gave you the gift of life on Earth.

You are a beautiful being and true beauty is not cosmetic, but arises from the depths of your being. Do not depend on others to reflect this great truth to you.

Be broad and generous in your embracing of beauty, for there is profound beauty in pain and suffering, too. Beauty lives in poignant farewells, in losses and letdowns, in longings and heartache, illness and ageing, even death, for these events can trigger the opening of your heart, the deepening of your understanding, the circulation of care and acceptance between you and others.

Embracing beauty will not shield you from sadness; it will not take away those feelings of inadequacy and isolation that are part of the human condition. But just as you admire the beauty of stippled light or a bronze-winged butterfly, an open fire or a simple stone, love too your wounds and sorrows. These are the vexations, the painful irritants which produce the pearls of self-awareness, wisdom and compassion which will make you truly, deeply beautiful from within.

As your life unfolds, keep the beacon of nature's beauty always within your sights – a clear jewel of water on a lily pad, the flute-like song of the pied butcherbird, the thick sunset mists that curtain your beach in moist mystery, a vein of pink quartz in a grey rock, the shiny, fragrant foliage of the lemon-scented myrtle tree. Nature's beauty is, I would remind you, love made manifest. Some beauty is ancient, some is transient, even momentary. Some is always at risk. And some, which has vanished into the black depths of extinction in your sphere, lives on in bright realities to which you're just beginning to attune. My power and mystery, which lie behind such earthly glories, also endure.

Your focus on beauty will help to magnetise you to me so that we may continue to work together for the highest good of the universe, so that through our partnership, the Earth and all her life forms may continue to blossom, blossom, blossom.

With love and light,

Mother Nature.

Songlines

The bush was dew-drenched, tinselled with spiders' webs and ringing with euphonic birdsong. My cheerful anticipation was well-founded, for the morning produced some rich encounters. During the mere hour I spent tramping through the wetlands, I came by willy wagtails, whimbrels, galahs, a grey-tail tatler, pied oyster catchers and pied stilts, heaps of seagulls, wattle birds and the ubiquitous miners, a little egret, a striated pardalote, a scarlet honeyeater, two fig birds, a flock of bar-tailed godwits (recently arrived from Siberia), black spoonbills (looking like can-can dancers with their feathers ruffled), elegant white-faced heron, pelicans, eastern curlews, little black cormorants, a mangrove gerygone, Lewin's honeyeaters, bar-shouldered doves, a grey fantail, a variegated wren, white-cheeked honeyeaters, brown honeyeaters, a pied butcherbird (with its flute-like notes, one of my favourite songsters), a southern fig bird, and a consternation of crows.

And then there were the ultra-shy birds I heard, but did not see. The distinctive whipcrack voices of eastern whip birds shot through the trees. In fact, this is antiphonal singing. Typically the male calls the first 'whip' notes and the female responds with the final emphatic 'choo choo'. This duet is so perfectly timed that it sounds like the performance of a solo singer. Occasionally when I listened patiently I would hear a delay in the reply, and this holdup, I learned later, was possibly because the female was swallowing an insect when her mate had called. Sometimes, when the female's reply is insufficiently prompt, the male will render the final notes himself.

I was also fortunate enough to spot a pair of ospreys – the female roosting in their huge nest of sticks on a man-made platform atop a disused telegraph pole, and her mate flying in with some slippery prey in his talons. Each river estuary can accommodate only one pair of osprey, which, these days, are endangered. Their numbers have been drastically reduced through the use of DDT which ends up in the sea and ultimately in the fish on which the birds feed.

Even a couple of yellow-faced honeyeaters, a formerly common species, which is beginning to diminish in this region, put in an appearance. In the 1960s, they flew over this region (which for much of its geographical history was a refugium for flora and fauna) in flocks of ten thousand. Now they, like so many creatures, are beleaguered by habitat loss. All is not entirely well in the estuary itself, either. From the 1980s onwards, fish kills became common and the local council in conjunction with the community continually review how to 'manage' the estuary.

Passing through melaleucas, banksias, wattles and hare's foot ferns defined and gilded by columns of morning sunshine, I lingered beside a cluster of paperbark trees in which dozens of rainbow lorikeets were feeding on the blonde blossoms. (Seeing lorikeets, I often smile as they remind me of the locals' term of endearment for my friend Rod Gibson – the

Poet Lorikeet of the Bay). The birds were inverted, their violet heads and their deep coral red beaks tucking in to their provender, their lime backs rounded; they hung superbly camouflaged like so many fluorescent avocados, except for their relentless shrill chatter.

But even *their* screeching was soon eclipsed by a large colony of laughing kookaburras whose full-throttle cackling was so raucous and prolonged, it rolled over me like a wave. A spontaneous laugh gurgled up from the low country of my own throat, and in that early morning mirth, in the thick of all that rowdy singing and wanton profligacy, those wild birds hit the bullseye of my joy, making a mockery of the 'modern prejudice that clarity cannot arise from profusion', making me realise that a sky without birds would be a barren sky.

Although 'very few birds share exactly the same markings', they do share something physical in common with humans: except in the hand region, the essential structures of the avian wing and human arm bones correspond exactly.

Plant life also shares a striking biological similarity to us. Or should we cite our similarity to them since they, according to science's version of how and when we all lobbed here, preceded us? Annie Dillard tells us that a molecule of chlorophyll comprises 136 atoms of hydrogen, carbon, oxygen and nitrogen 'arranged in an exact and complex relationship around a central ring'. At the ring's centre is one atom of magnesium. Extraordinarily, haemoglobin is *identical* to chlorophyll, except that its central atom is iron. Which means that we red-blooded beings are 'kissing cousins' to the green growths all around us.

It would have been dicey to try smooching up to one of those big-billed kookas, but I did not hesitate to wrap my (healed) arms around one of those tall, flaky cousins, a melaleuca. The bark fragments, fair tokens of the tree's benignancy, clung to my jumper, caught in my hair, and I gave thanks – for the life within me, for the healing I'd experienced (psychological therapy has 'no monopoly on the power to heal', as anyone who has lived close to nature will attest), and for the fact that the monolithic, international holiday resort formerly proposed for this site had not gone ahead, and the rich, natural lifeforms around me had thereby won a stay of execution.

I picked up a dead branch and headed for the beach. Although there was no sign of whales, they could well have been 'out there' in force for, as Rod has written: 'They sing to each other with eerie noises beneath the membrane of the sea.'

Walking the shoreline, I became aware that I was expectant, on the alert for *something* – movement, action, a flicker, a flash, a glimpse, a curiosity or distraction, a heart-expanding display, a defining moment. I have savoured the pep-ups, the ephemeral highs of such 'trips' (one overcast afternoon on my local beach I was thrilled to see a silver fish leap forward *five times* in high arcs; one evening, lying on the same sands, I saw a stunning succession of falling stars; one dawn a swarm of cobalt-colored bees blanketed the orange trumpet vine out back, and one sizzling spring high noon on deserted Tyagarah beach I was rivetted by a wallaby in the surf) and occasionally pine for more. In this grabbing mindset, how much of nature's subtle refinements and gradations can I appreciate, or even notice? Or more pertinently, how much do I miss? To how much am I oblivious?

During my perambulation, trailing the branch in the soft sand behind me, I caught myself humming, an aimless spill of jaunty notes that filled me up and at the same time made me feel lighter. My thoughts turned to the Aboriginal song-lines, those invisible pathways meandering across Australia: ancient tracks made of songs which tell of the creation of the land. It is an integral part of the spiritual fabric of tribal Aboriginals' lives to ritually travel the land, singing the ancestors' impassioned songs; singing the world into being afresh. In this way the land in all its guises, moods and incarnations floats through the plasma of their culture.

The Aborigines who still sing their land, sing not only to animals and plants, but also to the celestial bodies 'such as the sun, the moon, the Pleiades and some of the stars, and also to such natural phenomena as sun-heat, frosts, wind and rain'. Perpetuating the universe in this manner, the singers embosom not only those things which give life and gladness to humankind but also those things which create adversity and distress. 'Centipedes and scorpions, mosquitoes, flies and fleas, bull-ants and processional caterpillars, and the whole tribe of venomous snakes' are cited, too. As are dust-storms, whirlwinds and droughts.

Sharing in this unceasing work of renewing the universe, the whole tribe (and not just an elite group of holy ones) gains a sense of having a larger intention, a fixed design to bring to their own lives and to eternity. They believe that all the efforts of humanity are essential to maintain nature's harmonious functioning.

These days, many Westerners are hungry for such Dream Time songs, stories and myths; but tragically, in the genocide that took place after the white settlement of Australia, so many of the Aborigines' stories were lost[1]. Still, white Australians are overdue to discover our own ways of relating to the land, to find our own forms of spiritual transcendence. Wholesale 'lifting' of Aboriginal myths and totems from their original 'cultural soil vitiates their power' and is merely another form of plundering; it violates the Indigenous peoples as it diminishes the 'thieves', but not their estrangement from nature and its living spirit.

This set me wondering again about a riddle I'd been mulling over ever since my communing with Mother Nature began: Have certain stories, songs, wisdoms, always existed a priori in the earth's landscape or are they the projections, the inventions, of peoples throughout the ages? My instinctive response was that the former is true, a belief which I discovered (towards the end of writing this book) had been confirmed by James Cowan, an Australian poet and writer who has spent many years in the outback with tribal Aborigines. Cowan maintains that the landscape is imprinted with its own metaphysical or mythic data, waiting to be invoked. Even if we are wrong on this score, there are Eastern masters and Western theologians who maintain that projections during one's spiritual journey are essential, that without them the spiritual life (like love affairs) would not generate the heat to get started.

On the other hand, modern man's imprints and physical projections onto the planet are only too scarifyingly real – in the scouring of the land for metals, of the seas for food and oil, in the decimation of the forests, the poisoning of the waters with toxic waste, the staining of the sky with pollution and acid rain.

The poet and conservationist Judith Wright has been saying for decades: 'As Aborigines know, we live as part of a great interwoven net of dependencies, which cannot be broken without serious results to the whole, and in which we have acted as the destructive rogue factor. The Law which Aborigines recognise is one of kinship with the natural, and the environmental disasters which we have invited are disasters to that whole community of beings . . .

'However unpopular the word has become, I suggest that we need a recognition that we are part and parcel of a sacred organic order of kinship in which, whether we know it or not, we were born and live.'

———————

My Dear Child,

Those songlines you are contemplating are actually light lines made of sound. Like your leylines, they are lines of light, of sheer energy. They occupy their own place in the universal network of swirling forms, vibrations and transforming energies. The songlines, like everything in the cosmos are interwoven, inter-dependent, living and growing energies. They are part of the invisible reality underlying your physical reality, a reality in which the old delineations between form and substance, matter and energy, no longer apply, as your scientists are discovering.

If the relinquishing of old concepts of the world – like stasis and separation – unnerve you – you will always do well to turn to nature for help, for she is like a vast sounding board, a resonating chamber in which the vibrational wisdom of the universe, the sagacious music of the spheres, is held and ampli-fied. When the hunger for outcomes ceases to hog the limelight of your thinking, you may, through relaxing, letting go and letting be, rather than through concentrating or trying too hard, tap into her deep, untellably old wisdom, her creation and healing power, her spontaneity, vitality and strength, her freedom and mystery. And yet, paradoxically, to contemplate, to seek tranquillity in the arms of nature is an active, not an inert practice; it is one which requires a commitment of energy and intention.

When you access these inner resources, you affirm your own place within the complex web of life and at the same time become more self-reliant and self-referential. A flower does not require outward confirmation of its beauty, a mountain implicitly knows its own strength, the oceans do not question their colossal depths or worry about their alienation from the larger spiritual order.

So let yourself surrender to the solitude which fosters your conscious connection with the healing energy that resides in the Earth. Trust the wisdom and truth of the Song of Being as it echoes back to you (through the millennia) from a mountain canyon, an ocean shore, a forest, or from a single rock, leaf or creature. Through this silent communion, you are learning to be your own teacher.

If at first you hear only the top notes of the Earth's healing harmonics, do not worry, for only the Earth knows her own full, multi-planed score. There is no copyright, so provided you do not malign her, you may tune in to retrieve you own arrangement, however simple. Swelling orchestras can touch the soul, but so can simple a cappella.

When you let yourself go to these dimensions, you travel beyond individual imagination and into the realms of universal mind and wisdom. Wisdom is everywhere, inherent in all things, waiting to be discovered, revealed, unearthed. The wisdom of your own Dream Time is not a well-wrapped prize 'out there' waiting for you to collect and unravel it in some hazy, far-off mythic future; it is a dynamic knowingness available right here in this place where you are walking, right now in this moment, if you will permit yourself to fall into the crucible of quietude, the stillness of being through which it speaks.

The Earth registers every tread, every tender act and atrocity committed upon her face. Without judgement, she absorbs your goodwill or grief as readily as blotting paper soaks up spills of blue or red ink.

I am pleased to see you taking the time to become re-enchanted with nature, re-establishing a somatic sense of yourself as a small but key constituent of the Earth and enjoying the natural world for its own sake rather than for how it can be used or exploited. This kind of relating signifies the onset of a healing balance between your masculine and feminine energies, and the more balance you have between those energies, the more harmony you can create in your personal world. This personal harmony ripples out to the larger world and ultimately joins the rising green tide of human consciousness which esteems the critical value of the natural world, for its healing and perpetuation not only of humanity, but of all lifeforms.

With love and light,

Mother Nature.

1. It has been estimated there were between two and three million Aborigines living in Australia when the British arrived to found a penal colony in Sydney in 1788. By the time of the Bicentenary (1988), the Indigenous population hovered between 200,000 to 300,000.

Embracing the Erotic

Amid the Broken Head Nature Reserve, along Seven Mile Beach Road, there is a particularly high point which overlooks the sea. One of my favourite sites on the planet, it is majestic, Edenic.

For description, I cannot better the words of the National Parks and Wildlife Service: 'Before you is the heart of Broken Head. Rugged headlands, sandy beaches and rainforest. Notice how the vegetation follows the contours of the land, pruned and shaped by on-shore winds. Trees such as brushbox and tuckeroo flourish in these conditions, their crowns interlocking to form a protective shield or canopy which deflects the wind. From sheltered gullies, hoop pines emerge above the canopy. Bangalow palms – water diviners of the forest – grow along small creeks.'

One feverish summer's afternoon, wearing only my swimsuit (it was too hot for ordinary clothes or shoes), I stood on that dusty summit and let the trees and soil, the sand, surf and open space spark my curiosity: was this how things looked to the first man and woman who stepped foot on the earth?

The virginal vertú of the setting sent me spinning back

through history, communing again with entities long-gone from this earthly plane. All it took was a few lines verbatim and I was away. To the gaping, green ravine below me I reeled off a few of Duke Senior's lines from *As You Like It*:

'Sweet are the uses of adversity;
Which, like the toad, ugly and venomous,
Wears yet a precious jewel in his head;
And this our life, exempt from public haunt,
Finds tongues in trees, books in the running brooks,
Sermons in stones, and good in everything.'

Thus I summoned Shakespeare.

I said to him: William, I understand how you, a country boy and a fellow earth sign, 'knew much about birds and wildflowers, the weather, game and falconry'. But how did you at such a young age know so much about the idiosyncratic ways of men, women and the world at large? I've been to Bali and to Stratford-on-Avon, too, and I've seen Anne Hathaway's small bed. So if you would be so kind, tell me: in which enchanted forests of the mind and English countryside did you hang out to source your wisdom and witticisms, your ageless, incisive insights?

William cleared his throat and to me he did quoth:

'Our remedies oft in ourselves do lie,
Which we ascribe to heaven.'

'You may recall, my dear, that I gave that line to Helena in *All's Well That Ends Well*. That was four hundred years ago, and from my current vantage point it appears that human nature has changed very little since those good old days at the Globe[1].'

Another random stanza wafted through:

'There is a pleasure in the pathless woods,
There is a rapture on the lonely shore,
There is serenity where none intrudes,
By the deep Sea, and music in its roar:
I love not Man the less, but Nature more.'

This was penned by George Gordon Byron, 6th Baron, the British Romantic poet. (George's grandfather, John, was the Admiral after whom Captain Cook named our Cape Byron.) The younger scribe Byron also was noted for a long line of passionate and disastrous love affairs.

In his long satiric poem *Don Juan*, Byron wrote:

'There is a tide in the affairs of women,
Which, taken at the flood, leads – God knows where.'

In the sweeping solitude and engulfing silence of this spot at Broken Head, you can construct your own untampered-with screenplay. And so I slowly [DISSOLVED TO] Lord Byron, but not before I had thoroughly [FADED OUT] The Bard. I've been around the block a few times and one thing I've learned is that men enjoy confessional intimacy in each other's company about as much as cats enjoy being hosed down.

Lord Byron waited patiently in the ethers for me to address him, but I hesitated. Nothing would induce me to call him Lord.

Finally I said to him: George, excuse my psychoanalytic presumption, but no wonder your love affairs were disastrous. Goethe said you understood yourself 'but dimly', and you yourself wrote that you had 'no very high opinion of [women]'.

There is obviously some inner work to be done here,

George ... Now if you were living in this locus, at least you could sign up for a men's retreat to help you get in touch with the feeling intuitive in yourself, so you wouldn't need to project onto a succession of women, some as young as nineteen, your unattainable ideals. Why, who knows? A little drumming, a little chanting for a few nights could start to heal the emotional incisions made by your painful childhood, your vituperative mother, your club foot. The steady, pounding rhythms of the drums could help you to reconnect with the Great Goddess of the Eternal Widsom.

Recently I spotted a local promotional flyer for an upcoming men's event called ANCIENT VOICES: PATHS FOR MEN TO GROW WITH SOUL. It claimed:

'Men who are passionately alive are at ease with themselves and the world. This comes from a deep sense of connection to the web of life, a connection that flows naturally into appropriate action. Modern life promotes fragmentation and alienation that leads to depression, stress and bloody-minded aggression or passivity. Men live in a virtual reality acting like brains on a stick. This half-life values ''reason'' to the exclusion of intuition, common sense, imagination and feeling. It has left us lurching around, profoundly top heavy and unreasonable. It's time to come back to Earth.'

The flyer said the event would help men to

'learn how to turn stress into vitality through: * the ancient art of being here * finding your place amidst location and dislocation * healing the Soul in Nature * finding your way in the world *awakening to the soul and its link to the spirit and power of place * being fully embodied in action and repose * finding threads that weave your life story with world stories * discovering your rhythm and life pulse'.

So George, I segued, should you, per chance, decide to

beam yourself into my Down Under reality in time for that big North Coast corroboree of chaps, why don't you give it a go? It could steer you in the right direction, I reckon – and you never know who you might bump into later at the post office, the health food shop or the early morning tai chi class on the beach. Even if you don't 'get lucky', the $450 they're charging for the men's spiritual shindig still sounds well worth the splurge. Don't you agree?

At last I drew breath. George was silent. I persisted, pointlessly perhaps, but I couldn't help it.

George?

George said: Hmph, hmm and ah-ha, those familiar concessionary grunts which convey to a woman that she is 'but as the cuckoo is in June, Heard but not regarded'.

No long-suffering, white-knuckled hanger-on am I. A mere snap! of my fingers and I could [FADE BYRON TO BLACK], but at the instant I decided to do that, George spoke.

Inside the echo chamber of my imagination, I thought I heard him reply: M'lady, if a man calls out in the forest and no woman hears him, would he still be wrong?

And [FADED HIMSELF TO BLACK].

My privacy thus restored, I repeated another couplet from *Don Juan* as a mnemonic; ergo a roll of film footage of some of my own Don Juanian 'tides' unspooled through the darkened theatre of my mind. A number of them had been tsunamis by anyone's measurements. Memory is treacherously selective and will photograph, stagelight and frame according to disposition and desire. It can afflict or uplift. On this particular day a jump-cut trailer was projected, technicolourfully, on to the screen of recall – replete with smells, sensations and relived feelings. I felt my body being bathed in warm water and afternoon sunlight; saw amongst my damask bedsheets a beautiful, raven-haired being, the pentimento of his past just beginning to crease the satiny olive skin of his brow; felt my hair being brushed till my scalp tingled, my feet being massaged by fine-boned hands slippery with oil; smelt the natural sandalwoodish scent of his underarm. Through the ebb and flow of a long, collusive rapture, we mapped the contours of each other's desire to give and receive, to receive and be received. I saw myself swirling towards the dangerous 'destiny of type' – above and below, forward and back, this way and that, soft against hard, slower and faster, in and out, joyful and timeless; felt the fist of my heart unclench and heard myself moan into that much-loved man's mouth a torrent of pleasure; remembered thinking: *Oh God, he sees who I am*. And as he cried out, I felt an exquisite wave of energy wash through me, felt myself lifted as airily as a seed from the flimsy pod of my identity and spiralled out, out into some edgeless firmament, until I was a part of it, all of it, and I was lost.

Swept away in that reconvened rush of concupiscence, like a hierophantic empress of ecstasy, I was trying to divine whether to coo or cry, but there was no time to decide, for my naked thoughts were abruptly cut short when Emily came through.

She said: Perhaps you were right. Perhaps we should have written bodice rippers.

I laughed and countered: Well you did write: 'My business is circumference.'

Now you're trivialising me and taking me out of context! she snapped.

But, Emily, humour is an essential, playful part of eroticism. I'm talking loving, intimate, heart-expanding sensuality here, and you're coming across as stiff and self-conscious as . . . as a . . .

As a fence post?

As a bloke. Though sometimes the two can be disappointingly indistinguishable. Anyway, may I remind you, you did also write: 'Candour is the only wile.'

Well, that's true, she grudgingly conceded.

Not to put too sharp a point on it, Emily, but you did lead a much more sheltered life than me, so I feel it only fair to tell you: it's not necessarily always like that.

Like what?

You know – smelling the guy's sandalwood sweat, the long lost afternoons, the tender touching and all that. It's not like that for all of us all the time. It's not like that for most of us most of the time and it's nothing like that for some of us any of the time. Though if you've been tuning in to any of our popular culture, Emily, you could be forgiven for thinking that our sexual qualities are not only an aspect of our modern makeup, but the predominant or entire definition of it.

This proved too much for Emily, who promptly withdrew to her parlour, her Bible and thesaurus.

Paglia claims that Miss D, 'in her Sadean phase, [is] a blood-red moon of sexual will'.

Well not today, she wasn't. Perhaps Emily was just having an off afternoon, as we all do.

My Dear Child,

If I might have a word ... At this time in your Western culture, you humans regard sex and love synonymously. You have developed the belief that love and devotion will express themselves more deeply between you if you become adept at inducing female ejaculation, stroking the G-spot, pumping the prostate, pressing the perineum and other techniqued explorations of your loved one's anatomy. Yes, being sexual with another is natural and healthy for sex can open you up to love another being. Sex can open up the psychic channels. It can open up your heart, your mind, your outlook on life. It can help to attune you to the hidden realities, the higher senses. It can heal. Between loving partners, sex can be Holy. But if it becomes your only outlet for love, it is neither natural nor healthy.

You also have created an environment in which touching is equated with sexuality so that its natural occurrence on many occasions is inhibited by this taboo. Women learn that affectionate or lighthearted touching should not be indulged in unless it leads to a sexual climax and men learn to value themselves by their conquests and by the quota of sex they experience in any given period of time.

Love is not restricted to sexual acts or to society's prescribed notions of how often these acts 'should' take place in what your media insist on calling the 'average' person. There are no average people. Each individual is unique in his or her desires and needs and in the fluctuating expression of them. And as for love, it is the ultimate lawbreaker and rulebender. It wells up in every being and flows endlessly out into life in many different forms – through sexuality certainly, but also through kindness, creativity, prayer, conversation, humour, play. These are equally wonderful, valid expressions of the essential, exuberant eros of living in your physical reality.

With love and light,

Mother Nature.

*   *   *

Speaking of eros ... As Sandy from the motel might say: I do not wish to cast nasturtiums (or should that be fig leaves?) onto the unfortified male psyche, so I will let a few of the more self-informed fellas fling their own male-female philosophies around ...

Scott Wetzler writes: 'Not only do I listen to "war" stories from patients about the men they love, live or work with, but I read about openly passive-aggressive[2] acts in the press, relating to politics or business, stories that intrigue me about manipulative men who negotiate the boardroom and bedroom with equal effectiveness ... The Women's Movement created a tidal wave of identity crises, male and female; women want the opportunities men always had open to them, and push for them; men want what they always had – the power – but they give it up or do not give it up, [often] passively-aggressively. Macho isn't dead, just a bit comatose.'

Peter Bishop remarks: 'As if in direct response to fears of a devouring Great Mother, Australian men have an unenviable reputation with the feminine and women, one in which sexual uncertainty goes hand in hand with aggression and disdain.'

Ronald Conway claims that 'Australians have so often tried to conduct their emotional dealings with the land and with others through the slit of Ned Kelly's armour. With rifle, football boot or penis cocked, we have constructed ourselves in images of winners or losers, of misplaced heroisms and wasteful sacrifices. It seems time to drop Ned's armour and realise that the enemy has been mostly within our ego-selves.'

Matthew Fox is more blunt: 'As a man I have to ask, are we men totally devoid of the erotic? Or do we only act as if we were? Construct MX missiles and Trident submarines and make ''war games'' as if we were? Who will redeem us men from our compulsion to control the erotic, to banish it to unhappy bedrooms, to stifle it in boardrooms and classrooms and say that truth comes from ''clear and distinct ideas'' and footnotes and budgets and price lists – but not from celebration?'

Fox is on to something. And so is Audre Lorde in her eloquent and pertinent speech, 'Uses of the Erotic: The Erotic as Power'[3]. Lorde liberates eroticism from its modern, narrowly defined context of hormonic convergence and relocates it where it really belongs – in its broadest, unabridged and truest sense – as the abstract, wide-ranging principle of desire, as a profound depth of feeling (not a passing sensation), as a passionate celebration of life. Eroticism has been misappropriated by the multi-billion dollar pornography industry and, in this remorseless theft, its wider appreciation and expression has been virtually annihilated and lost to our Western, patriarchal culture. Matthew Fox concurs with Lorde that a 'feminist spirituality as distinct from a patriarchal one will value the erotic and teach us disciplines of erotic celebrating, creating and justice-making'.

Here is what Lorde said:

'There are many kinds of power, used and unused, acknowledged or otherwise. The erotic is a resource within each of us that lies in a deeply female and spiritual plane, firmly rooted in the power of our unexpressed or unrecognised feeling. In order to perpetuate itself, every oppression must corrupt or distort those various sources of power within the culture of the oppressed that can provide energy for change. For women, this has meant a suppression of the erotic as a considered source of power and information within our lives.

'We have been taught to suspect this resource, vilified, abused, and devalued within western society. On the one hand the superficially erotic has been encouraged as a sign of female inferiority – on the other hand women have been made to suffer and to feel both contemptible and suspect by virtue of its existence.

'It is a short step from there to the false belief that only by the suppression of the erotic within our lives and consciousness can women be truly strong. But that strength is illusory, for it is fashioned within the context of male models of power.

'As women, we have come to distrust that power which rises from our deepest and non-rational knowledge. We have been warned against it all our lives by the male world, which values this depth of feeling enough to keep women around in order to exercise it in the service of men, but which fears this same depth too much to examine the possibilities of it within themselves. So women are maintained at a distant/ inferior position to be psychically milked, much the same way ants maintain colonies of aphids to provide a life-giving substance for their masters.

'But the erotic offers a well of replenishing and provocative force to the woman who does not fear its revelation, nor succumb to the belief that sensation is enough.

'The erotic has been misnamed by men and used against women. It has been made into the confused, the trivial, the psychotic, the plasticised sensation. For this reason, we have often turned away from the exploration and consideration of the erotic as a source of power and information, confusing it with its opposite, the pornographic. But pornography is a direct denial of the power of the erotic, for it represents the suppression of true feeling. Pornography emphasises sensation without feeling.

'The erotic is a measure between the beginnings of our sense of self, and the chaos of our strongest feelings. It is an internal sense of satisfaction to which, once we have experienced it, we know we can aspire. For once having experienced the fullness of this depth of feeling and recognising its power, in honour and self-respect we can require no less of ourselves.

'It is never easy to demand the most from ourselves, and from our lives, and from our work. To go beyond the encouraged mediocrity of our society is to encourage excellence. But giving in to the fear of feeling and working to capacity is a luxury only the unintentional can afford, and the unintentional are those who do not wish to guide their own destinies.

'The internal requirement toward excellence which we learn from the erotic must not be misconstrued as demanding the impossible from ourselves nor from others. Such a demand incapacitates everyone in the process, for the erotic is not only a question of what we do. It is a question of how acutely and fully we can feel in the doing. For once we know the extent to which we are capable of feeling that sense of satisfaction and fullness and completion, we can then observe which of our various life endeavours bring us closest to that fullness.

'The aim of each thing which we do is to make our lives and the lives of our children more possible and more rich. Within the celebration of the erotic in all our endeavours, my work becomes a conscious decision – a longed-for bed which I enter gratefully and from which I rise up empowered.

'Of course, women so empowered are dangerous. So we are taught to separate the erotic demand from most vital areas of our lives other than sex. And the lack of concern for the erotic root and satisfactions of our work is felt in our disaffection from so much of what we do. For instance, how often do we truly love our work?

'The principal horror of any system which defines the good in terms of profit rather than in terms of human need, or which defines human need to the exclusion of the psychic and emotional components of that need – the principal horror of such a system is that it robs our work of its erotic value, its erotic power and life appeal and fulfilment. Such a system reduces work to a travesty of necessities, a duty by which we earn bread or oblivion for ourselves and those we love. But this is tantamount to blinding a painter and then telling her to improve her work and to enjoy the act of painting. It is not only next to impossible, it is also profoundly cruel.

'As women, we need to examine the ways in which our world can be truly different. I am speaking here of the necessity for reassessing the very quality of all the aspects of our lives and of our work.

'The very word ''erotic'' comes from the Greek word ''eros'', the personification of love in all its aspects – born of Chaos – and personifying creative power and harmony. When I speak of the erotic, then, I speak of it as an assertion of the life force of women; of that creative energy empowered, the knowledge and use of which we are now reclaiming in our language, history, our dancing, our loving, our work, our lives.

'There are frequent attempts to equate pornography and eroticism, two diametrically opposed uses of the sexual. Because of these attempts, it has become fashionable to separate the spiritual (psychic and emotional) away from the political, to see them as contradictory or antithetical. "What do you mean, a poetic revolutionary, a meditating gunrunner?" In the same way, we have attempted to separate the spiritual and the erotic, reducing the spiritual thereby to a world of flattened effect – a world of the ascetic who aspires to feel nothing. But nothing is farther from the truth. For the ascetic position is one of the highest fear; the gravest immobility. The severe abstinence of the ascetic becomes the ruling obsession. And it is one, not of self-discipline, but of self-abnegation.

'The dichotomy between the spiritual and the political is also false, resulting from an incomplete attention to our erotic knowledge. For the bridge which connects them is formed by the erotic – the sensual – those physical, emotional, and psychic expressions of what is deepest and strongest and richest within each of us, being shared: the passions of love in its deepest meanings.

'The considered phrase, "it feels right to me," acknowledges the strength of the erotic into a true knowledge, for what that means and feels is the first and most powerful guiding light toward any understanding. And understanding is a handmaiden which can only wait upon, or clarify, that knowledge, deeply born. The erotic is the nurturer or nurse-maid of all our deepest knowledge.

'The erotic functions for me in several ways, and the first is in the power which comes from deeply sharing any pursuit with another person. The sharing of joy, whether physical, emotional, psychic or intellectual, forms a bridge between the sharers which can be the basis for understanding much of what is not shared between them, and lessens the threat of their difference.

'Another important way in which the erotic connection functions is the open and fearless capacity for joy. In the way my body stretches to music and opens in response, hearkening to its deepest rhythms, so every level upon which I sense also opens to the erotically satisfying experience, whether it is dancing, building a bookcase, writing a poem, examining an idea.

'That self-connection shared is a measure of the joy which I know myself capable of feeling, a reminder of my capacity for feeling. And that deep and irreplaceable knowledge of my capacity for joy comes to demand from all of my life that it be lived within the knowledge that such satisfaction is possible, and does not have to be called marriage, nor god, nor an afterlife.

'This is one reason why the erotic is so feared, and so often relegated to the bedroom alone, when it is recognised at all. For once we begin to feel deeply all the aspects of our lives, we begin to demand from ourselves and from our lives' pursuits that they feel in accordance with that joy which we know ourselves to be capable of. Our erotic knowledge empowers us, becomes a lens through which we scrutinise all aspects of our existence, forcing ourselves to evaluate those aspects honestly in terms of their relative meaning within each of us, not to settle for the convenient, the shoddy, the conventionally expected, nor the merely safe.

'During World War II, we bought sealed plastic packets of white, uncolored margarine, with a tiny, intense pellet of yellow coloring perched like a topaz just inside the clear skin of the bag. We would leave the margarine out for a while to soften, and then we would pinch the little pellet to break it inside the bag, releasing the rich yellowness into the soft, pale mass of margarine. Then taking it carefully between our fingers, we would knead it gently back and forth, over and over, until the color had spread throughout the whole pound bag of margarine, leaving it thoroughly colored.

'I find the erotic such a kernel within myself. When released from its intense and constrained pellet, it flows through and colors my life with a kind of energy that heightens and sensitises and strengthens all my experience.

'We have been raised to fear the yes within ourselves, our deepest cravings. For the demands of our released expectations lead us inevitably into actions which will help bring our lives into accordance with our needs, our knowledge, our desires. And the fear of our deepest cravings, keeps them suspect, keeps us docile and loyal and obedient, and leads us to settle for or accept many facets of our oppression as women.

'When we live outside ourselves, and by that I mean on external directives only, rather than from our internal knowledge and needs, when we live away from those erotic guides from within ourselves, then our lives are limited by external and alien forms, and we conform to the needs of a structure that is not based on human need, let alone an individual's. But when we begin to live from within outward, in touch with the power of the erotic within ourselves, and allowing that power to inform and illuminate our actions upon the world around us, then we begin to be responsible to ourselves in the deepest sense. For as we begin to recognise our deepest feelings, we begin to give up, of necessity, being satisfied with suffering and self-negation, and with the numbness which so often seems like the only alternative in our society. Our acts against oppression become integral with self, motivated and empowered from within.

'In touch with the erotic, I become less willing to accept

powerlessness, or those other supplied states of being which are not native to me, such as resignation, despair, self-effacement, depression, self-denial.

'And yes, there is a hierarchy. There is a difference between painting a back fence and writing a poem, but only one of quantity. And there is, for me, no difference between writing a good poem and moving into sunlight against the body of a woman I love.

'This brings me to the last consideration of the erotic. To share the power of each other's feelings is different from using another's feelings as we would use a Kleenex. And when we look the other way from our experience, erotic or otherwise, we use rather than share the feelings of those others who participate in the experience with us. And use without consent of the used is abuse.

'In order to be utilised, our erotic feelings must be recognised. The need for sharing deep feeling is a human need. But within the European-American tradition, this need is satisfied by certain proscribed erotic comings together, and these occasions are almost always characterised by a simultaneous looking away, a pretence of calling them something else, whether a religion, a fit, mob violence, or even playing doctor. And this misnaming of the need and the deed gives rise to that distortion which results in pornography and obscenity – the abuse of feeling.

'When we look away from the importance of the erotic in the development and sustenance of our power, or when we look away from ourselves as we satisfy our erotic needs in concert with others, we use each other as objects of satisfaction rather than share our joy in the satisfying, rather than make connection with our similarities and our differences. To refuse to be conscious of what we are feeling at any time, however uncomfortable that might seem, is to deny a large part of the experience, and to allow ourselves to be reduced to the pornographic, the abused, and the absurd.

'The erotic cannot be felt secondhand. As a black lesbian feminist, I have a particular feeling, knowledge, and understanding for those sisters with whom I have danced hard, played, or even fought. This deep participation has often been the forerunner for joint concerted actions not possible before.

'But this erotic charge is not easily shared by women who continue to operate under an exclusively European-American, male tradition. I know it was not available to me when I was trying to adapt my consciousness to this mode of living and sensation.

'Only now, I find more and more woman-identified women brave enough to risk sharing the erotic's electrical charge without having to look away, and without distorting the enormously powerful and creative nature of that exchange. Recognising the power of the erotic within our lives can give us the energy to pursue genuine change within our world, rather than merely settling for the shift of characters in the same weary drama.

'For not only do we touch our most profoundly creative source, but we do that which is female and self-affirming in the face of a racist, patriarchal, and anti-erotic society'.

My Dear Child,

I have some things to say about all that, but they can wait. Go home now. Make yourself a fine meal.

Carrot juice, lots of carrot juice, fresh papaya and a few vegetables with rice would be good for you at this time. I invite you to return tomorrow, just on dark. Come deep into the rainforest, to where the fireflies dance, and I shall talk to you about women, men, passion, love and where we're all heading.

With love and light,

Mother Nature.

1. Shakespeare went to London, first as an actor, and then as actor manager, he was involved with Richard Burbage in the Globe Theatre.
2. The term 'passive-aggressive' was first devised during World War II by an army psychiatrist, Colonel William Meninger, to describe the way enlisted men tried to cope with the structured conformity, compliance and absence of personal choice imposed on them by the military. Many soldiers 'resisted orders, withdrew or simply wanted to flee'. Menninger called this resistance 'passive-aggression' and classified it as 'an immaturity reaction'.
3. Lorde's speech was published as a pamphlet and later included in a collection of her writings, *Sister Outsider: Essays and Speeches*, published by The Crossing Press, Inc., Freedom, California.

The Dance of the Fireflies

Fireflies, those tiny nocturnal beetles, use their 'lights' to find mates.

Where does their light come from? I'd always wondered. A little research revealed that firefly light organs are usually located on the underside of the abdomen. A chemical reaction which takes place in the light organs produces the firefly's own, generally greenish, bioluminescence. Some species of female fireflies wait on the ground until a male nearby flashes the correct signal. She then answers him with her own light signal. In other species, the flying male, which may itself be nonluminous, is attracted to the female's light. Common in warm and tropical regions, the adults live for between five and thirty days, feeding on nectar or fresh air.

Deep in the gloaming of the cool rainforest, I crouched amidst the fireflies, dozens of them, flashing, signalling, illuminating, converting the leaf mulch, ground cover and understorey into a fairyland with their viridescence, their crepuscular charm.

It was the perfect setting for wild imaginings, so I dwelt awhile on Audre Lorde's ideas, trying to envisage how the world might turn if enough of us began to enact them. It seemed to me that if we are to heal the psychic and emotional ravages and rifts between men and women, between mind and body, between the earth-defiling industrial order and the earth-worshipping environmentalists, between the economic rationalists and the artists and mystics, between the debased erotic and the creative-spiritual erotic, between the personal and the political, between the masculine and feminine principles in ourselves, between how we have been conditioned by our technological age to aspire, achieve, live, labour and love, and how, given a different societal structure, we would truly, madly, deeply prefer to do all those things (if we could but pause for long enough to consider alternative choices): in short, if we are to heal ourselves and ipso facto the planet, then we could do worse than implement some of Lorde's recommendations in our lives. Day by ordinary day. Step by daring step. All it takes is courage (which in the French, Chinese and Maori languages means 'big heart') – and courage is not the same as endurance.

The psychic and physical splits in our world at this time run deep, and little will change until mass consciousness changes. It all starts, as it must, with the individual. Have you ever watched a flock of water birds for any length of time? Gliding sedately on the surface of the water, they look as if nothing would ruffle their repose. Yet it takes only one bird to beat its wings and pretty soon the entire flock will start flapping and fluttering, only to lift up in one beautifully blended ascription.

Theodore Roszak puts it another way. He calls it 'the song of myself'. This song may be little more than a short jangling tune, but 'sung by a sufficient number', it is enough to start mending the deep splits, 'to halt the rhythm of the great machine ...'

Jung saw our life purpose as being to work towards uncovering and becoming more of who we authentically are. Roszak goes further: 'In becoming even a small piece of ourselves, we become what the burdened planet needs: creatures with some more urgent calling, some greater joy than comes of waging war upon nature.'

It is easy to take cheap shots at the self-discovery phenomenon that has been building up amongst ordinary people across the planet since the baby-boomers hit the scene. It is simplistic and convenient to call people's preoccupation with self-knowledge 'narcissism'. But, as Roszak points out, those firing the shots 'hear the desire to be treated as special and unique and they call it self-indulgence. They bemoan the buzz-words on the surface, failing to attend the desperate need beneath. Shall we say they "pity the plumage, but forget the dying bird?"'

Yes, I, too, cringe at the crass mass marketing of mind, body and spirit, at the bizarreries, the psychobabble, the distorted distillations of deeper truths, at the proselytising New Age neophytes (and they are as rampant as lantana around here) who, uninvited, lay their poultices of newfound 'wisdom' – slap! – on the psyche of the nearest living being. Like the satirist said: 'A little learning is a dangerous thing.' Yet in this pervasive shift in societal direction, I share Roszak's view that it is of 'great political, personal, and ecological value ... It is the brave beginning of a project that both the person and the planet require ... If this be narcissism, make the most of it.'

Ah, but my thoughts have spirited me, as they often do, away with the fairies, and Mother Nature is waiting in the wings to talk to me about men and women, about the way we are and the way we might be.

My Dear Child,

You humans often remind me of those little fireflies you are sitting amongst. I see so many of you frantically flashing your lights, earnestly looking for the perfect life partner instead of learning to become a partner with life.

For a long time in your planet's history, the union of the male-female was for the perpetuation of the species. But, unlike the fireflies, you don't require that any more. You already have many more people on this planet than you need. So now the truer sense of the male and female union is one of equal partnership. And I do not mean two halves coming together to make a whole, but rather coming together to experience a sense of sharing.

It is indeed time to heal the painful splits between men and women on this planet. To start with, men have to re-learn – as they once knew in much earlier times – how to open their hearts and not just their sexuality to women, to respect and honour women's wisdom, their creative contributions, their bodies. This shift in attitude goes hand in hand with honouring the Great Mother – the Earth, for the healing of the two are inextricably linked.

And you women have to give up your anger at men, to start to melt the steel in which you have encased your hearts for protection ...

Let's look for a moment at creation as a whole. On the earth plane there was a decision made to explore creativity in a separation of frequency, or supposed separation of frequency. And thus a woman was made and a man was made. Literally the frequency is the same, but one is a more defined frequency in terms of masculine and one is a more defined frequency in terms of feminine. So the differences between the masculine and feminine frequencies are quite great. And thus the differences between the male and female are quite great. Now in your world you are beginning to understand that though they are different in their frequencies or manifestations, they are actually still two parts of a whole. Dwell on this a while, for its seeming contradiction can stretch your narrow concepts of male, female and the whole corporeal kit and caboodle.

Because of the way the world has worked up until now, the two parts of the whole have been either:

1. The feeling of incompleteness if you weren't with one – which isn't the truth because you are very whole in and of yourself. Or:
2. The resentment that half of yourself is still outside of yourself and that you actually might need that experience.

Those are both distortions of truth – because the truth is: there is one being. It is just as if this is a right hand and this is a left hand. They are very different and yet they are still connected. But what has happened is that on the earth plane, people have not seen the connection. That comes from understanding the nature of creation. So man has wanted to define his wholeness by separating from woman and woman has wanted to define her wholeness by separating from man. And so a lot of that need for separation has created the great gaps in communication between the genders.

Now it is time for this communication to be resumed. Now in your experience of wholeness. Not because you women were mad at men. Not because they hurt you. But because during the separation you gained an experience of your wholeness. Now you women can take that wholeness and begin to communicate to a man. Not as if he's separate from you. And not as if he is the other part of you. But rather that he's just another experience of creation. It is important for you women to start communicating with men again. This is the most important thing for you to do. Start communicating – not from your protection, for that is not a very deep place – but from the place of who you really are.

I encourage you to begin to witness that part of yourself that does not wish to let a man in on that deep level any more. You could tell yourself, for instance: 'Well I'm noticing that I'm relating to this man as if there's no depth there. And that's because I don't want to show my depth to him.' And then you may reconsider: 'Well, I'm willing to show a little bit more of my depth to him.'

Because really you women do desire to relate deeply to men again, as they do to you. But many of you – both genders – are holding secret the place in your hearts that desires to relate to one another again.

Breathe deeply into your heart where that gap is. Because right now so many of you can very much feel the vacuum in your hearts. You can feel the child who wants the love of the father or mother. And then you can feel the defensive adult who says: 'I'm not letting them get to me.' The truth lies beyond the child and beyond the adult; it lies in the soul who came here to understand creation.

So start working with that gap in the heart between the adult who says: 'You guys/girls are not gonna mess with me any more.' And then the young child who says: 'I just want you to love me daddy/mummy, no matter what I am, no matter what I do.'

And then begin to feel the variance of the space between those two frequencies, and start being willing to put your beauty in that space between this child who desperately wants nothing but love and this adult who says: 'You're not going to hurt me.' Do you follow me?

There is a big space between those two frequencies. Neither of those is your true essence. But both of those are designed to teach you the difference of who you appear to be, versus your true essence. And I see that many of you are now ready and willing to become that.

While I have your ear, I'd like to say that you women and men have got to learn to develop your own wholeness and sense of security – and doing this is an inside job. You don't need a man or a woman to help you to know who you are. *Know* who you are!

And call forth a man or a woman to share in your own lusciousness. See that you are full and full from within yourself. Need nothing outside yourself to confirm your worth and identity.

It hasn't been time for many of you women to be with men yet because you are learning so much. You are in a great time of change. You are longing to be less structured, more fluid, more organic, more sensual. You want to be able to perceive more subtly and to experience the subtle energies ...

Now, about these fears that you all have – women and men – that you won't find union with another being ... Have the knowingness in yourself that that which you perceive as a potential is not a pipe dream. Nor is it a fantasy that you have been fed from the outside world. It is a deep inner yearning and knowing in your soul self that it is capable of that level of union you have been dreaming of.

And yes, I understand that your society believes that you are doomed and destined not to be in a relationship if you don't have one by about thirty-five. But that is not the truth. Through developing your consciousness, you humans are making radical changes in your relationships. And actually, now the better relationships will be those which are formed in the late forties. Because it is during the first forty years that people go through their childhood or infancy experiences on the earth. And then they can come together and have much more of an expanding or a blossoming. Your minds keep telling you: 'It's too late.' But it's not. Your lifespans are increasing and there are so many of you who have agreed to be part of this transformation, this growth towards wholeness.

(By the way, I see that in recent times, you personally, until you actually began transcribing my letters, wouldn't really have wanted a man because you would have ended up using your creative power for him.)

Meanwhile, I do encourage all beings to open yourselves up more to having friends. And just acknowledge: 'I'm really needing a woman – or a man – as friend. I'm really needing to relate to a woman/man.' Many people are finding themselves in that position at this time. They are needing to know who they are in relationship to the opposite physical form.

So, as a woman, try to be willing to have that. Without the fear that the male form will hurt you.

I worry that men will get in the way of my creativity . . .

They won't get in the way. They'll only enhance it. It's like the flower saying that the bee is in the way. They go together. The flower could not replicate itself if it were not for the bee.

And although the flower, like you, thinks: 'This creative process is coming from me,' you're going to need a man to help you distribute that book. You're going to have to work with men to get it published. So it's for you to start working, not from the adult who protects and not from the child who needs, but to develop the understanding that there are some things that the male can do that the female has not

194

done. And that is alright. Because there aren't too many men who could sit in the garden with me and hear me transcribing letters to them ...

With love and light,
Mother Nature.

Assorted Armageddons

It is easy to forget, especially when you live in a city, just how potent and *alive* nature is and how, so it appears, we are shackled to, and at the mercy of, the natural world. Nature can be 'red in tooth and claw,' as we are regularly reminded by news bulletins about floods, bushfires, droughts, cyclones, earthquakes, landslides, tidal waves.

Natural disasters make compelling copy, an example of which appears in *Time and Tide*, a history of Byron Bay. The Bay was once a seaport and had a flourishing fishing industry. That was, until nature intervened ... The town's first jetty was built in 1888 and was regularly overhauled until 1928 when a brand new jetty was constructed. This second jetty featured 'two electric cranes enabling vessels to load on either side'. All went well until February 1954 when a cyclone hit northern New South Wales.

'When news of its projected path was known, the fishing fleet was lifted by the cranes onto the outer section as was the custom in such conditions. That night, the fishermen went to bed thinking their boats were safe, but the next morning when they awoke, their boats were gone, along with the outer section of the jetty, the electric cranes and all other gear. Twenty-two boats in all had disappeared and with them went the end of Byron Bay's fishing industry ...

'Today the jetties have gone. The remainder of the old jetty was removed in 1947 and the remnants of the new one were removed about 1974. If you look closely today at low tide you can still see the broken ends of the piers of the old jetty opposite Jonson Street.'

One autumn not so far back, torrential rain, high winds and heavy seas battered the north coast for a week. As reported in our local paper, *The Echo*, more than 750mm of rain fell on parts of the Shire during that time, some Byron shops were flooded, the highway between Mullumbimby and Brunswick Heads was cut and helicopters made emergency drops of food to families stranded by rising floodwaters in Upper Wilson's Creek.

In my relatively protected garden, the wind had shredded and whipped the foliage till it was black and raw. One pawpaw tree keeled over, but I managed to save two others by tethering their slender trunks to the fence with fabric slings.

When the downpour finally stopped, I took the instant antidote to the sub-tropical strain of cabin fever and ventured out to the beach, or what remained of it. Heavy seas had pounded and decimated the dunes. A five-metre casuarina lay prone. Among its roots were the clumped remnants of the sand in which only the day before it had been so firmly planted; its foliage was still a thriving green. In the dune regeneration area, the young plants dangled their filigreed roots from the precipice of a five-foot sandbank freshly hacked by the waves. No trace of any ambient serenity there. The beach had been brutally gashed to a narrow, grey strip and the sky was still scabby with storm clouds. Yonder at the Cape, three hang gliders zapped about like tiny mosquitoes sucking ineffectually at the brooding air's blood. If I had to give Mother Nature a face then, it would have been scowling, menacing. Yet even this louring seaside scene, with its battered and bruised landmarks, held an irresistible appeal, a creative freshness. The lugubriously exciting evidence of the unexpected lay all around me. As Barry Lopez says: '... sudden cataclysmic events are as much a part of life, of really living as are the moments when one pauses to look at something beautiful'.

Standing in the shallows that indigo evening, I felt the tide rush up and swirl around my ankles and calves. Just as quickly it receded, churning and dragging the sand swiftly, unpredictably from under my feet. It took concentration to hold steady, to remain centred and balanced in the centre of that watery turmoil. When the tide ebbed again, my feet were planted more deeply, yet more tentatively in the sand. In the lull before the next wave brought dissolution, I closed my eyes anticipating the surge, allowing the ocean's lusty volatility to sweep through me, feeling the moving mounds and willing hollows of grains, flimsy and malleable as tissue paper. All was permeable and nothing was permanent. Then the next wave heaved and broke, dousing me with its blue and white promise of inevitable change.

The body of the planet, of course, is not the only entity caught in the momentous changes and upheavals at the dawn of the new millennium. As Thomas Berry says: 'All the human modalities of being that have existed in the past are being profoundly altered. We ourselves are being changed. ... Just as the planet is changing more than it has changed in such a long period of time, so the human order that brought about this change is being called to alter itself in an equally profound way'.

No longer can we 'deductively get our guidance from the past,' advises Berry. 'There is, in a sense, a new revelatory experience that has given us a new sense of the universe, a new sense of the planet earth, a new sense of life, of the human ... The universe story is the quintessence of reality. We perceive the story. We put it in our language, the birds put it in theirs, the trees, put it in theirs. We can read the story of the universe in the trees. Everything tells the story of the universe. The winds tell the story, literally, not just imaginatively. The story has its imprint everywhere, and that is why it is so important to know the story. If you do not know the story, in a certain sense you do not know yourself; you do not know anything.'

Berry maintains that if we are to sustain ourselves and future generations in a 'mutually enhancing relationship' with the earth it will take 'a spiritual discipline that involves a change from our anthropocentrism to a biocentrism and a geocentrism. It will even require a move from democracy to biocracy.'

Right now humanity needs, according to Berry, 'the sagacity, as well as immense energy, to find our way into the Ecozoic[1] era. People say we cannot do it, and the answer is that we *must* do it. There are sacrifices to be made. There is the discipline. There is the spirituality. There is a divine meaning in the process. If we do not perceive the sacred nature of our journey, then we will not be able to bring about the salvific transformation needed. We need to appreciate especially the real dimensions of what it is to be a member of the sacred community in this larger sense of the term.'

The natural world is broadcasting to us, loud and clear, what we must do. And the natural world is one of the great mediums through which the Divine speaks to us.

____

My Dear Child,

I have some preliminary insights to offer you. There will be more to come later, but for now I wish to remind you that I am Mother Nature, benign, benevolent, all-giving, yet ever-changing, who did birth you all.

On land and sea and in the air, I am simply doing, as I always have done and always will do, what comes naturally. I am self-organising, self-regulating, self-maintaining, self-perpetuating – and upheavals of great magnitude are part and parcel of these processes. Whether these upheavals are held to be part of my beauty or my terror is a matter of perspective.

It may appear to you that I deliberately or indifferently wreak savage, violent, tragic consequences, but this is not the case. I do not have punishing designs on the human race. During the untellably long multiple lives of the cosmos, I, Mother Nature, have never played favourites, for I vitalise every speck and species in your universe.

I do not judge the sudden processes and complex interactions which collectively contribute to a living, evolving planet. All of my processes – from the tiny breeze generated by the flapping of a butterfly's wings to the almighty surge of a tidal wave – hold equal significance for me. Each one is part of the

200

patterns and inter-relationships between all things on Earth.

Every day I am full of fluctuations and turbulence, some of which your human eyes cannot even see. The clouds that look as inert as cotton wool are in fact seething and tumbling through the air, the waves roll in and break in rhythms that never repeat themselves. Certain species preponderate and decline at different times. Disequilibrium is an essential ingredient in *my* harmony, which is almost never static.

Your conventional view of harmony as *orderly*, is limited and hangs like a dense cloud over your consciousness. For in all destruction there is creation; upheaval is integral to harmony and can also bring forth great beauty. Look at Uluru, for example, nobly thrust up in the midst of that vast flat terrain; and the rich green of your home territory was birthed during the eruption and lava flows of so long ago.

The Earth's surface changes continuously, spontaneously, and there is an inherent order and purpose in these changes which you, with your neat little ideas about order, seldom perceive. The agents that altered it in the past are still at work today, but because some of them operate very slowly, you tend to lose sight of them. In essence, there are two – water (rivers, tides, and so on) and subterranean fire (which produces earthquakes and volcanoes).

I am calling to so many of you now, not only to enter into a partnership with the Earth as it exists in this moment in time, but also through the power of your desires, thoughts, beliefs and intents, to facilitate all lifeforms to continue to undertake their natural reproductions, transformations and evolutions.

At the same time, I encourage you to relinquish the belief that humankind is an aberration or a villainous blight on the planet and that some day in the far – or near – (depending on the level of your pessimism) future, you will extinguish yourselves and the natural world. You are in a dynamic state of spiritual evolution and despite evidence to the contrary, the pure essence and intent of humankind is toward the good.

You need not ignore the warfare or the damaging of the physical environment (though even these acts spring from the misguided belief in their good intent). But I do recommend that you focus on and act from the empowering experience of my unimpaired unity and wholeness which is everywhere around you, if you will but attune to it. Allow your senses to drink in my unimpeachable virtue and soundness. Allow these qualities to succour and uplift you and to dominate and mould your thoughts and beliefs which, during your every breath, create your realities on this plane of existence.

With love and light,
Mother Nature.

While Mother Nature's letter appeased me to some degree, it left me with an itch of curiosity about what she would offer in her next, advanced instalment.

Meanwhile, I couldn't help but notice how the Earth and its climate are changing – sometimes proportionally, sometimes violently – in response to the changes which humankind is inflicting on her. We cannot go on burning and slashing the forests, gouging the earth for minerals, poisoning the atmosphere, drilling beneath the sea for fossil fuels; we cannot change the biosystems, the geology, the ozone layer, the very fabric of the planet, without 'natural' repercussions. I ruminated myself into a fug.

I was doing just what she'd asked me *not* to do – becoming fixated on and anxious about imagined disasters that might never eventuate, wondering where it all would lead, when Mother Nature appeared to me in a dream. I found myself deep in a forest. From the earth, I picked up a decaying leaf and held it up to the light. The glossy green glamour of its treebound life had long left the leaf, which was now a mere outline of a flat brown blade. Yet through the delicate network of its remaining veins, fine, brittle and fast fading; through its unbearably beautiful lightness of being, shone the radiant white energy of another realm. This light, which I instinctively identified as Mother Nature, pierced me with knowledge:

My Dear Child,

You need to recognise that nature's cycles (*including* humankind) occur within a larger framework of understanding ...

And then I saw a book with a pinky red cover, whose title I could not quite decipher ...

In waking life, time, that loopy revoker of linear law, apparently, went by. One day I travelled to visit a distant friend, and while she was in the kitchen making a meal, I scanned her bookshelf, keen, as ever, to check out the kinds of thoughtful company others choose to keep. From the tightly packed shelf I freed a few tomes whose titles caught my eye. One was a Seth book: *The Individual and the Nature of Mass Events*. In it, I found the larger framework of understanding to which Mother Nature had alluded:

'Your most advanced thinkers emphasise man's rape of the planet, or focus on the future disaster that will overtake the world, or see men once again as victims of the stars ...

' "You get what you concentrate upon." Your mental images bring about their own fulfilment. These are ancient dictums, but you must understand the ways in which your mass communications systems amplify both the "positive and the negative" issues ...

'The dreams, hopes, aspirations and fears of man interact in a constant motion that then forms the events of your world. That interaction includes not only man, of course, but the emotional reality of all earthly consciousnesses as well, from a microbe to a scholar, from a frog to a star. You interpret the phenomena of your world according to the mythic characteristics that you have accepted. You organise physical reality, then, through ideas. You use only those perceptions that serve to give those ideas vitality.'

Humanity, Seth insists, is 'a part of nature, and a part of nature's source'. Seth explains that:

'The officials of the Roman Catholic Church altered many records – cleansing them, in their terms, of anything that might suggest pagan practices, or nature worship as they thought of it. In terms of your civilisation, nature and spirit became divided so that you encounter the events of your lives in that context. To some degree or another, then, you must feel divorced from your bodies and from the events of nature. The great sweeps of emotional identification with nature itself do not sustain you, therefore. You study these processes as if you somehow stood apart from them ...

'You think of rain or earthquakes as natural events, for example, while you do not consider thoughts or emotions as natural events in the same terms. Therefore it is difficult for you to see how there can be any valid interactions between, say, emotional states and physical ones.

'You might say: "Of course, I realise that the weather affects my mood," yet it will occur to very few of you that your moods have any effect upon the weather. You have so concentrated upon the categorisation, delineation, and exploration of the objective world that it surely seems to be "the only real one". It seems to exert force or pressure against you, or to impinge upon you, or at least almost to happen by itself, so that you sometimes feel powerless against it ...

'It seems quite clear to you that the mass events of nature are completely outside of your domain. You feel you have no part in nature except as you exert control over it through technology, or harm it, again through technology. You grant the weather has an effect upon your moods, but any deeper psychic or psychological connections between you and the elements strikes most of you as quite impossible.

'... You use terms like "being flooded by emotion", however, and other very intuitive statements showing your own deeper recognition of events that quite escape you when you examine them through reason alone. Man actually courts storms. He seeks them out, for emotionally he understands quite well their part in his own private life, and their necessity on a physical level. Through nature's manifestations, particularly through its power, man senses nature's source and his own, and knows that the power can carry him to emotional realisations that are required for his own greater spiritual and psychic development.'

As for the prospect of humanity extinguishing itself, Seth remarks: 'Only an objectively tuned consciousness like man's would imagine that the physical eradication of a species destroyed its existence.' Species, like viruses, he explains, 'exist in the earth's memory, to be recreated, <u>as they were before</u>, whenever the need arises'.

Like a seasponge, I absorbed all that, and much much more. I took solace from Seth's assertions that the personal impulses we are frequently taught to view as dangerous, chaotic, or contradictory are instead crucial to the best interests of the species and the natural world, for they lead us to live 'not only as loving caretakers, but as partners with other species'.

Reading the Seth material took me back to one of Mother Nature's earliest proclamations to me:

'And this is really what your writing is to be about. Helping people to understand that everything is designed to work perfectly ...'

1. Berry claims we are nearing the end of one biological age, 65 million years of the 'lyric' Cenozoic Age, and are in the process of entering another which he calls the Ecozoic. The Ecozoic, he says, demands that we rethink all our human institutions, honour our sense of interconnectivity with all living things and come out of denial to deal with our massive ecological devastation. The Ecozoic age also asks us to develop fresh understandings of science, technology, ethics, language, education and religion. Berry predicts the Ecozoic age will be 'governed by the arthetype of woman' in contrast to the patriarchial dominance of the dying Cenozoic era. See recommended reading for further information on *Befriending the Earth*.

Rising and Returning

Each day before I start to write, I light a candle and ask for the highest good to flow through my work, whatever form it may take, writing or reading or staring out the window for who knows how long. One day towards the end of winter, I stared for a long time at the candle. It was a dark blue one, burned about halfway down, its flame still strong and tall. As it burned, it did not drop any wax onto the candleholder. Inch by inch the wax disappeared, like magic. Abracadabra. Now you see it. Now you don't. Where did the wax go? Did it devolve naturally into nothingness? Did it transmogrify into some invisible form of ether and hang around?

For the duration of its life, that candle lit up the room in which I write and dabble, burn bergamot oil and daydream, and all the while I was aware it was burning itself into oblivion. Did it know, or even suspect its ultimate destiny? Or was it too intent on each second of its own sticky survival to entertain that purple prospect? Second by second, its flame stretched and contracted, rose and fell, flickered and bent in the slight breeze. In an hour or two, all that would remain to remind me of what it had offered the world was a shred of charred wick.

Meanwhile, its gentle radiance held me entranced. I looked and looked at that blue candle which had burned itself halfway to nirvana or heaven knows where. I stared and stared at the flame, and the intensity of my focus, paradoxically, began to melt the mutterings of my mind, to disentangle me from the chainmail of the corporeal. I drifted and drowsed until the rest of the room diffused and blurred, then vanished, until all my thoughts extinguished themselves and I slipped effortlessly through some etheric opening on the other side of which all concept of a personal 'I' was lost, irrelevant. I became amorphous, boundless, a draught of pure nothingness, floating simultaneously inside and outside the flame's golden dance, merging with its unpredictable dips and sways until I *was* that flexible flame, I *was* that half-gone candle, and that candle was me. And 'time' was a foolish figment of some poor, mad world's imagination.

When a freakish gust of southerly wind blew in, stirring the pile of loose papers on my desk and sending half of them flapping to the floor, I snapped – Voila! – back into the tension of my body sitting straightbacked on the typing chair, my eyes roving the plain, pink wall. Wryly, I thought: at the risk of rashly misidentifying all of us (thanks to Elton John) with Marilyn Monroe or Lady Diana (even golden goddesses must 'As chimney-sweepers, come to dust'), each of us is, essentially, a candle in the wind.

By some 'immortal hand' we are formed, moved about, strategically placed to add color or design – temporarily – to the world. We are lit up and left to burn our own bright and trembling way through this life. Exposed to too many ill winds, we may temporarily or prematurely fade out. But for however long we are ignited we have the chance to bring to our time here whatever capacity for warmth and illumination we have gathered down the line. And when we finally snuff out, our remains may be interred or scattered over land or sea. Then our flames will rise up in other realms and time will be obliterated until we decide to offer ourselves once again to that materialising hand, to return to increase our understanding about this particular reality in which we shine, to offer once more our services to this beloved blue planet.

*   *   *

One afternoon in early spring, I packed a small picnic basket with two more blue candles, with two coloured photographs, a posy of impatiens and cat's whiskers from my garden and two pieces of writing. On this day during the previous year, my friend Catriona and I had gone to the Cape to burn candles and say prayers of gratitude and goodwill for Neville and Lancelot, the cats we once knew and loved, and who died on the same day, three years apart. If you live for long enough with a pet, inevitably you become deeply attached to him or her, and the sad truth is that we almost always outlive them.

After they die, they leave behind a poignant gap which, depending on what is happening in your life, you may or may not choose to fill with another creature. Anyone who has ever loved an animal will understand. The shared life and love, the loss and subsequent bereavement can be no less intense than what we feel for our homo sapiens loved ones, for love does not discriminate among species. Or let me put it another way: blood is not necessarily thicker than water. It's just stickier.

So ... I went alone to spend the afternoon at the Cape (as Annie Dillard exhorts us: '*Spend* the afternoon. You can't take it with you.') for Catriona reluctantly had left the lotus-eating way and gone to sojourn, to earn by writing for a while in the land of mammon in the south. Her presence, particularly on that day, was sorely missed.

Up at the Cape the light, even on a partly overcast day, was mercilessly intrusive. The verve of the place was so dynamic, I felt like a chance motif in that cinerama, my presence vestigial, almost swallowed up by the uninterrupted vista. Across the face of the planet the sky was stretched like a clear blue membrane, a sentient skin tattooed with clouds, some as fine as eyelashes, others as lush as mermaid tresses or a lion's mane. Janus-faced, I looked from land to sea and back again, unabashedly stealing succour at every turn. The place defied any symbolic or psychological decoding and I am no autocued oracle. There would be no ventriloquising today. Sometimes a Cape is a Cape is a silent green thumb of land, offering nothing emblematic beyond its own iconic veneer and clean airborne scent. But neither did I pry for more. I was content to enjoy the rich photo-realism of the place, the scattered highlights – the lighthouse, the white guard rails, the bursts of yellow-blossomed bitou bush – that perforated the predominantly pastel scene. The demarcation between light and shadow was smudged. This fuzziness, together with my sense of being dwarfed, tipped my equilibrium: no matter how accomplished our own living artistry, mostly we are afforded only a hazy or sectional view of the Big Picture. Head tilted back, I stood revering the sky as the seventh and final veil of mystery, but as G. Evelyn Hutchinson has written: 'The biosphere does not end when the light gives out.'

A brahminy kite appeared out of nowhere, as birds will. It hovered directly above my upturned face and, if I was not imagining it, made prolonged eye contact with me. Fascinated by this encounter, I waited – neck uncomfortably angled, eyes

210

watering from the glare – until the bird flew off. Then, as agilely as one of the wild goats which for so many years lived on its steep inclines, I picked my way down into the protected northern crook of the land and sat on the thick grass. I lit the candles, lay the two feline photographs alongside the flowers, took out the papers and began to talk to two cherished memories who have moved on to make merry elsewhere.

'My Darling Neville, My Little Orange Man; Handsome Man; Ruby's Little Brother; The Boy; The Mechanic,

'So many names, so many roles. Too many roles for one cat – brother, son, court jester, spiritual advisor, family nurturer, marriage guidance counsellor, wise old man of the hearth, great jungle hunter – *scapecat*.

'Dear boy, you were the one who remained calm in emotional storms, steady amidst insanity, loyal in the house of infidelity. You were the one we all relied on and, as I lost the others, one at a time, as I lost myself to grief and despair and madness, you became the *only* one I could rely on. You became my everything. Far too much for one little cat.

'The psychic said – "Our children and our animals love us so much they die for us." It comforted me for some time to think you proved to be the hero I always knew you were.

'I can't believe it's so long since that terrible day you died. Your little face is so clear in my mind's eye. And your ways – you loved your bikkies in the morning and your hearts at night, you liked to shake one of your back legs after a little drink of water, then you would give a brisk, regal wave of the tail and skip out your cat door, sort of squeaking as you went, as if to announce – "I'm off for my evening inspection now, expect me when you see me."

'I can still feel the sensation of my finger sinking into the softness of that hidden fur between the padding of your paws and I can feel the vibration of your purring engine when you slept on my back, or on my chest. Remember when I came home from India, jet-lagged, and slept for sixteen hours? You stayed with me the entire time. I have a picture of us, me snoring on my back, you on my chest, guarding me, soaking up the reality of my presence. Rejoicing in my return. Sometimes, I would wake up and your face was in my face and we purred together, just loving each other.

'We loved each other so much, we felt each other's pain. I nearly died that time your paw got jammed in the car door. The door was locked. You were screaming. I was screaming, but I had to keep myself together to unlock the door with a key held by hands that just wanted to faint.

'In the end, it was my pain that made you want to die. All that pain, that remorse, that sheer, utter terror you must have absorbed while sleeping on my back or crouching by my side as you did, for hours and hours, on the back step. I drank red wine by the cask and endlessly, relentlessly tried to sort out the universe in a cloud of dopey smoke. You waited and waited for the light, but it just got darker by the day and you had a new role – a new burden, as the reflection of my soul. Too much for one little cat.

'That psychic – he also told me I would have a love affair with a very funny man. Very funny!

'My darling boy, you didn't die for me, you died *because* of me. I'm so sorry. Please forgive me.

'Catriona.'

Beloved Lancelot,

When I was aching and worn with loss, and beginning to believe that in the night all cats are grey, you came into my life – a tiny, fluffy, fun-filled streak of silver-grey.

An envoy, an omen, I hoped, of better times to come. And in a way I was right, for you proved to be one of my greatest teachers, capable of the kind of unconditional love we bipeds talk about, aspire to, but seldom actualise.

In those early days, I had no idea of the journey we would embark on together.

I remember with sheer delight so many things about you that gave me joy.

I remember your silvery back gleaming in the sunshine and the softness of your ivory belly.

I remember your dignity and fair grace.

I remember your sweet voice and your need to communicate at all hours of the night and day. Like me, Lancelot, (you were never a generic 'Puss') you always enjoyed a bit of a chat.

I remember how you preferred classical music, but you tolerated it when I played rock songs, too.

I remember how we used to sit on the back step and eat custard for breakfast.

I remember how you waited to greet me on the front doorstep whenever I arrived home.

I remember how we played hide and seek inside that little cabin.

I remember your pure, sweet smell and your spontaneity in play.

I remember the gifts you brought me from the garden. Thanks to you Lancelot, I'll never be afraid to deal with rats – dead or alive – again.

From you I learned it was possible, even in repose, to have an unrelentingly sensual zest for life.

You were a master of ease, centredness and indolence. In

fascination, I watched you, my beloved exemplar, but remained a poor pupil. In recent times, however, I've been learning to cultivate langour.

I remember times when I was ready to give up, had it not been for your presence and constancy, your devotion and unconditional love.

I remember the time I lay grief-stricken on the bed and you jumped up on my chest and comforted me; licked my third eye and drank the tears from my sad woman's face.

But more than that, I remember your essence, your blithe and generous spirit.

I remember how true you were to yourself.

Exactly who was depending on and learning from whom, waxed and waned between us. Let the urban psychologists mutter about emotional displacement and the outsiders make jokes about *Catdependent No More* – till the cows come home. I know we were brought together to cooperate and learn from each other for our own evolutions and for that I can only give thanks.

I'll never know what took you off to the Great Shining Spirit of the big back paddocks, but I understand that it was personal choice, and not some unpredictably cruel kismet. And yet, I can tell you, beautiful boy, some mysteries weigh heavily on the human heart.

Still, the enigma of your passing unveiled for me some secrets of living. Your departure was a gift to me because the grief over your loss forced me to live in the moment and to face the aloneness which every human being must sooner or later – and sometimes repeatedly – confront.

We shared some expansive times together and I shall always recall them with gratitude.

Since you passed on, Lancelot, I've seen the living light in the eyes of every animal I encounter – and that is a gift and a blessing rich beyond counting.

'Shelley'.

Shakespeare observed drolly: 'Men have died from time to time, and worms have eaten them, but not for love.' Yet love, as the great poets and Shakespeare himself knew, is the ultimate gift, the highest blessing. Sitting up there at the Cape, I felt a blessing welling inside me, warm and comforting as freshly baked bread. I was pondering how to give voice to it when a pied currawong flew by, wailing in its loud, falsetto voice 'crik, crik, bewaiir!' A song. It came to me to sing a song. Of all my choir's repertoire, *Shine on Me* is my favourite tune. We have sung it for years – in rehearsal, at weddings, concerts, parties, protest meetings – and I never tire of it. To me it is a simple yet potent blessing song.

Up at the Cape on a quiet day, you can sing in your own Sound of Music and no earthly being will notice. So I started to sing it softly as a blessing for Lancelot and Neville, for Catriona and me, for the people we love dearly and, as the singing made me vaster, for the ones we love less, for the one's who've wounded, for surely, I reasoned, they needed blessing, too. As I crooned softly, a rapid stream of images of one and all and all as one flowed through my mind. So I sang on and on, for the currawongs and the brahminy kites, for the earthworms and the Aborigines, for the ocean and the great open spaces of Terra Australis, for all the creatures and people on the planet and for Mother Earth herself. I kept repeating the brief lyrics until I was satisfied that everything and everyone I could encompass in my mind, feelings and spirit had, by the grace of All That Is, been blessed.

'Shine on me, Shine on me,
Let the light from the lighthouse shine on me.'

*   *   *

'All things are in process, rising and returning. Plants come to blossom, but only to return to the root. Returning to the root is like seeking tranquillity. Seeking tranquillity is like moving toward destiny. To move toward destiny is like eternity. To know eternity is enlightenment and not to recognise eternity brings disorder and evil. Knowing eternity makes one comprehensive; comprehension makes one broadminded; breadth of vision brings nobility; nobility is like heaven. The heavenly is like Tao. Tao is the eternal. The decay of the body is not to be feared.'

Lao-Tse

Next day, down in the back forest I was gathering fallen branches and adding the snappy twigs, together with vegetable scraps and newspaper, to one of the compost heaps. The two heaps were breaking down beautifully, turning into dark, worm-rich soil, which I was in the process of turning when Mother Nature came through.

My Dear Child,

The cycle of life-death-life is endless. All transformation entails a 'death,' a passing from one form into another.

If you watch the life cycle of a fruit tree, first the

216

buds break out; then they open fully into blossoms; next the fruit appears, drops to the ground decomposes and fertilises the earth and the cycle goes on. These are essential occurrences in a ceaseless cycle of wholeness. Most humans don't see the whole life cycle.

There will be cycles when you are very actively composing your life (your self-expression, your relationships) and cycles when the form of it is decomposing. The same happens with your body. You go from being an infant to being an adult, and in old age, often return to more childlike states again.

In your cycles of dying (whether that be in old age or much sooner) many of you become frightened of or angry about the decomposition of the body, and that is natural. But you, dear one, who is working so deeply with nature, seeing every day composition and decomposition, seedlings growing into plants, plants blossoming, shedding, breaking down, going back to compost, you are beginning to understand and accept that decay and death are natural and essential parts of this great cycle of energy. Your parents give you life. They nurture you and you blossom. Then they start to shed, and as they do, you continue to blossom. One day your time to decompose arrives and whoever or whatever it is you have been able to nourish, blossoms while you wither and decompose. And so it goes on, this beautiful cyclic journey which you humans are only just starting to appreciate. You are just beginning to understand there are realms beyond logic, materiality and intellect, and that death is not the end of the journey, it is merely another continuation, one which guarantees the ongoing vitality of the species, for as your friend Seth says: 'Death prunes the planet.'

The time will come when this decomposing happens to those close to you (and ultimately, of course, to you, too). If they seem afraid, you might try to console them by advising they surrender to this phase, to trust that the unchanging essence of them will survive the death of the physical body. You might tell them that in their passing, a part of you also will die and that that part will accompany them on their spiritual journey. In speaking to your loved ones about these matters, you are emulating me who speaks to you and reminds you that you do not travel alone.

It is natural for you as a child to want to take care of your elders. And it is important for you, who with the passing of the years, become more a parent to them than a child, to understand you cannot alleviate the fear and pain they may experience in their own transitional process. If they deny belief in a spiritual dimension, then in some ways all you can do is let them know on a vibrational level that decomposition is part of nature. You can look at a loved one with eyes that say: 'I know your soul, beloved. I know there are many places we can go. This is just one of them.'

It is for you to learn to hold and share those truths so that your loved ones might die, as far as is possible, with equanimity. It is possible to die peacefully. Peace, however, is not passive. Peace is potent power. Peace is a choice and does not depend on outer circumstances.

There comes a time when each being yearns to be free of the flesh and move on to a new framework of existence and learning. The soul yearns for the death of the body, just as it once yearned for its birth, and this is a natural and healthy desire which can arise at any age. No plane crash or landslide, no terrorist's bomb or aids virus will claim the life of a person who, at some very deep level, has not chosen to die.

As for your animal friends, they have a more instinctive understanding and acceptance of all that happens to them during the living and dying of their physical form. A relationship with your pet provides constant opportunities for deep reciprocal learning, and often they are the less resistant pupils in these matters. They can be among your greatest teachers, if you will allow them. Having consciously chosen to evolve through living close to you, animals generously bestow on you their natural power to understand and imaginatively enter into your feelings. Just like you, they are striving to increase their ability to feel. Equally, they sometimes decide, in full awareness, to take in or assimilate some of your human illnesses and emotional pains. They have an intense affection for you and do not resent this; they experience it gladly, for it is part of the spiritual exchange they entered into in opting to be with you. Since they are capable of willingly receiving what life dishes out to them, they agonise over their setbacks less than human beings. Because you humans nearly always outlive your pets, they give you the chance to witness and experience most poignantly the life-death-life cycle. Soon after they have passed from the material world, your pets, just like your human loved ones, may visit you in your dreams to reassure you that they are living and thriving in other dimensions.

Beloved child, somewhere deep down you already do know these things to be true. All of you know much more than you allow yourself to think you know, but too often you are playing a hide-and-seek game involving yourself and your gurus and deities. You hide your own vast wisdom under a bushel and then try to extract it from others. Some of you believe that the more dollars you pay, the better the guidance you acquire. It is necessary sometimes to seek help outside, but remember: always look first under your own nose for truth and wisdom.

So often you forget about self-referral. You let yourself fall asleep at the wheel, so to speak. You get lazy. You feign amnesia. You want to be let off the hook about something. You want someone else to tell you how things are, what you should think or say or do. But in many instances you are only pretending not to know. In that huge hive of humanity in which you live, each of you, every woman, man and child can be the queen bee of your own honey dreaming if you will but listen, really listen to your own innate wisdom.

With love and light,
Mother Nature.

26

The Rainbow Season

Chasing rainbows around here is actually not such a long shot, for the rainy season is also the rainbow season. During sunny breaks, I'm inclined to head for the beach, rain jacket at the ready, hoping to catch an afternoon moodlifter over the sea, The Cape or Broken Head, since rainbows appear in the direction opposite to the sun.

A rainbow is a rainbow is a gorgeous gestaltic trick of the light, I'd always thought, but it turns out there can be several tricks – the primary, secondary, tertiary and supernumerary rainbows.

So I discovered one rainy day in our local library, that under-funded, overcrowded, damp-smelling repository of so many surprises and amazements. About rainbows, the *World Encyclopaedia* had this to say: 'The brightest rainbow is the primary bow, and the secondary is sometimes visible outside this arc. Its colour order is reversed from that of the primary – that is, red appears on the inside and violet or blue on the outside of the secondary bow. A third bow, called a tertiary bow, is sometimes seen outside the secondary bow. It is produced from three internal reflections, and its colour order is the same as that of the primary bow. The colours of secondary and tertiary bows are increasingly less intense than those of the primary bow. In fact they often appear as only bright bows of white light'. Supernumerary rainbows, said the *Encyclopaedia Britannica*, were 'faintly coloured rings' which were 'seen just inside the primary bow. The[se] owe their origin to interference effects on the light rays emerging from the water droplet after one internal reflection.'

So theoretically, I reasoned, it should be possible to see a quadruple rainbow. In the city I'd seen more rainbows in brake fluid than in the atmosphere. In Byron, I'd seen double rainbows all over the shire, and several years ago at one of my weekly choir rehearsals, three tenors had arrived like raving magi, bringing the good news of a triple rainbow over the Mullumbimby canefields. But a quadruple! Now that would be some celestial sideshow.

After I finished my library readings, I strolled up to the beach which, on account of the weather, I had virtually to myself. En route I passed three parked cars with MAGIC HAPPENS! bumper stickers and recognised them as locals. At the T-intersection near the surf club, a large magpie with a mouthful of detritus, strode matter-of-factly across Fletcher Street just as an oncoming, old ute stacked with furniture, turned into it. In anticipation of the imminent splattering of blood and feathers on the bitumen, I peeked between the fingers I'd clamped over my contorted face. The driver braked just in time and I removed my hands from my face to see the bird cross nonchalantly to the other half of the street where a bicyclist in faded tie-dyes swerved nimbly around her. The cyclist doffed a battered Akubra, first to the maggie and then to me as I stood mouth agape with relief on the pavement.

'We all gotta live here, don't we?' the cyclist called out.

'We sure do. I didn't recognise you under that big hat.'

It was Sandy, from the motel.

'Being careful. Already had two big melaleucas burnt off my face.'

That must have been some burn, I thought, and, raising an arm in salute, I turned again towards the beach, comforted by the fact that through the years and the briefest exchanges, Sandy's endearing malapropisms flashed almost as brightly and dependably as the lighthouse.

There were no full rainbows that afternoon, but a chunk of one on the horizon snared my interest, rising like a half-formed genie, an opalescent gift from a celadon sea. Gifts, I thought. Gifts ...

On the wet sand, a cluster of gulls squabbled over a scrap of bread. Somewhere in me their screeching sounded a wake-up siren signalling what a gift it is to listen, not merely to hear, which is a passive activity, but to involve the body, mind and psyche in tuning in, focussing. (Ninety percent of brain stimulation comes through our ears. Sound readily travels around solid objects, while light doesn't.) As I paced along, I began to make a short list of some of life's greatest gifts to me. Few of them, it emerged, could be scientifically explained or even proved to exist, yet all of them had imprinted themselves on the receptive mind. The soaring of my spirits through singing, the silent pauses that make music the moving medium that it is, the dulcet noises of nature, the givenness of love, the elegant if unnerving symmetry of synchronicity, the enigmatic exhilaration of art, the heart-opening power of humour, the ethereal ecstasy of dreams, the fateful intervention of intuition, the primordial aegis of light ... I was just warming up when the purple heavens parted, pelting polka dots down onto the sand and my bare head. I shrugged. This communing caper could be chancy. I was too far along the beach to race for shelter, and besides, it was only wet, not wintry. So I sloughed through the sand and thought some more about earthly gifts in all their reflected glory. Sometimes we may give a gift (of time, tenderness, of listening without judgement, a pot plant or a poem, whatever) and although we may not receive from that person, yet we may receive from elsewhere. It is, as Lewis Hyde, put it, 'as if the gift goes around a corner before it comes back'. We have to give blindly, says Hyde, and we will 'feel a sort of blind gratitude as well'.

That afternoon my gratitude lingered in the full glare of the stormy light which, as we're told, travels in straight lines. If light could bend around corners, as P.W. Atkins points out, 'the world would be harder to discern. It would be like listening to it instead of seeing it. We would be immersed in a symphony of colour from objects that could be vaguely located but only hazily scrutinised. There would be no night; the symphony would be endless.'

Like light that travels as a wave, giving and receiving follow their own undulations, their own secret series of peaks and troughs. It occurred to me that somewhere along the divinely overlit paths of my who-knows-how-many lifetimes, I must have given a good stash, for here I was on a wet weekday afternoon, mentally tramping through the inventorial wonders of the ones which had boomeranged back to me. The pleasure of that privilege slid all around me, as fleet and slippery as mercury.

Trying to spread it around a little longer, I decided to play I-Spy. Pick a letter, Ready, Go! 'S.' Stone sand shoreline shells surfer. 'W.' Go! Water wings waves wagtail. 'P.' Go! Petrel paper plastic (oh-oh). 'C.' Go! casuarina crab crag clover castle (on four levels detailed with stones shells and feathers complete with moat and just about to be battered by a wave) cream sand clean air (Okay. Okay. Adjectives are cheating).

My game was interrupted by a barking blue heeler up ahead. He sniffed the sand, stepped sideways quick-smart, then barked again. Approaching him gingerly, I saw that he was treading on a nest of tiny bluebottles which had washed up on the shore. (If you're an inattentive clodhopper, as I'm sometimes prone to be, the transparent creatures burst like plastic bubble-wrap underfoot.) The blue heeler stepped on a few more. They went pop! He went woof! And I laughed and laughed.

By the time I reached cover, it was, of course, unnecessary, for I was euphorically wet, my hair flattened into raggedy ringlets, my skin singing with the tears of attention from that eye, the sky.

My Dear Child,

I'm glad to see you giving thanks for some of the natural world's many gratuities, for when you do this you automatically begin to align yourself with the creative current that pervades your world of matter. When you drop into this contemplative focus, you are intrinsically recognising that in body and soul you are one with the Earth, with the Divine and with all of creation.

Speaking of which, the Divine has given you your own gifts and waits patiently for you to express them.

There is a time to be idle, to go within, to plunge into the deep mysteries, to seek the inner light, 'to turn on, tune in and drop out' as you all said back in the flower-power days. In this time of jettisoning your old lifeform, you may wish and trust that the Absolute will give you a fair trade, a compensatory 'something' for what you have given up. And then there comes a time to return to the outer world, to bring back with you some token of what you have gained from the in-dwelling time; this is the time of speaking out, of gift giving, of sharing with others the shards of light you have glimpsed amid the transformative abyss into which you dived.

Like every human being, you come in to your physical world with certain gifts and it is one of your highest purposes to use them.

So many of you have great beauty to express in the world, but you are not doing that. You have buried that creative expression somewhere in your subterranean depths and are standing fearfully on the surface of your life, hiding behind a smokescreen of security and 'Yes, buts'. Consider this: there is a world of difference between, say, five years of experience and doing the same year five times.

Perhaps you are afraid that your efforts will not be rewarded or will not measure up to others' expectations. Dear child, you don't express yourself in order to win others' approval; you do it because this is the essence of who you are! In your world it has been decreed that this passion for expression attaches itself only to those who are acknowledged as great leaders in their chosen fields. But this passion belongs to everyone. It is passion for life! And that is what creative energy really is, isn't it?

When you fully express your creativity, it is as if you are sending rainbow light back through the very lightwaves that have created you. So allow yourself to see in your heart that this is true fulfilment – to receive the total spectrum of love and light, to circulate it within your being and then to send it right back out into the universe. *This* is how you become a co-creator.

I encourage you to celebrate play and imagination in all forms. Enjoy your own creative faculties! Embrace your creativity, spontaneity and freedom to express. Look with wonder upon these qualities. They are agents of transformation, gifts, without strings, from Creation to you.

For some of you, it can take a long time for your desired vocation to manifest. In the meantime, however, trust that everything that happens to you serves to prepare you for what you will bring to the world later on. And in the meantime, trust the impulsive flow of your life. Keep in mind that you, like every individual, have the power to make a difference to life on Earth, not through grand, sweeping actions in the future, but by small, steady shifts in attitude and behaviour wherever you are Right Now! For example, you may be in a job where you're required to reach certain targets of income or production – tangible or intangible – for your employer. That is the nitty-gritty of your work. But there is always another level at play in your daily activities. Perhaps you are in that position to learn patience, structure, humility, compassion, cooperation, trust. You may be a parent learning through love of your children to stretch your capacity to give. You may be running your own business in order to learn to be of service to others, your staff or your customers; to make them laugh when times are grim or to inspire them. A thousand different reasons. The same applies to the entire spectrum of your life. Every experience – the delightful as well as the disappointing or even the grisly – is, if you will allow yourself to see it that way, grist for the mill of your personal expression and contribution to life on your physical plane.

Wherever you find yourself, whatever you are doing, know that you *are* on your correct path. Indeed, it is impossible *not* to be on your path, even if it sometimes looks like you got detoured on some corrugated, overgrown backtrack. Trust that it *is* leading you somewhere and give it your best shot.

In the meantime, check out, if you can, what you really enjoy. What really matters to you? What excites or pleases you? What makes you wonder? Or weep? Or feel immeasurably richer? What makes your soul sing? When you find what it is, then you can bring your whole being to its expression.

It is essential to practise, to watch how others in your field do things, to take note of their triumphs and failures. But you cannot seize the gift of your own artistic bequest to the world through discipline or willpower before it is ready to be made manifest. If you try to grasp the form or the physicality of it too soon, it will elude you as surely as a rainbow.

Sometimes there needs to be a long process of life experience, of personal fulfilling before you can give voice, shape, colour, texture, sense or meaning to that deep desire to express. If you try to force it to fruition too soon, you may indeed create something, but it will be like those tasteless tomatoes in your supermarkets. It will have a pale glow, but will lack the authentic, rich taste of uncorrupted seed which has been nurtured and ripened in nature's full cycle.

Remain receptive and the creative way will gradually reveal itself – in glimpses and impressions – in a snatch of conversation overhead, in the lyrics of a song on the radio, in a flare of personal anguish, in the afterglow of a sunset, in the melody of a magpie, in a magazine image, in a deep knowingness in meditation.

Never let your own instinctive wit and warmth be crushed by the conventional wisdom of how things 'should' be done. Whatever your form of work, do it from love and the desire to give of your best. No matter what sort of work you do, – whether it be simple or sophisticated, humble or high-flying, concrete or intangible – these states of mind inevitably will be reflected in its integrity. Painting a watercolour is a gift, but so is the way a fruiterer arranges his grapefruit and green vegetables to display them at their most luscious and appealing, or the caring way a nurse treats a dying patient. Every being is equally capable of becoming a channel for the Divine. Its flow through you depends on your pure intent, your unselfish desire to give, on your receptivity.

There comes a time when, through surrender and acceptance, those aspects of your psyche and outer life which you previously perceived as a punishment or a painful burden, you begin to perceive as blessings, as ingenious re-routings towards spiritual growth. This tricky transmutation – which can take years to complete and which must incorporate that mysterious, quintessential ingredient of alchemy, the 'divine spark' – is one of the greatest gifts you can give to yourself and to the world.

If you cannot incorporate your preferred form of creative expression into your work yet, then start by expressing it through a hobby or pleasurable pass-time. Play with it and let this play help you to begin to understand the nexus of creating by an inspiration. I stress the concept of *playing* rather than regarding your hobby as a direct bridge to 'what's next'. Through play, you will revive the experience of how and why you love to create and you will strengthen your sense of identity as a creator.

Do not focus on the glittering prizes – the money, the acclaim, the status. Their inflationary rewards are mere passing shadows of the real body of gratification, which encompasses your life impulse, your desire, the generosity of your desire, to blossom and then give a gift back to the universe which gave you the greatest gift of all – your life.

With love and light,

Mother Nature.

27

____

Tribal Voices

In the clefts of Bangalow Road as it ascends steeply and scenically towards Hayter's Hill, the larger birds are nearly always to be seen riding the anabatic air currents with a style that looks decidedly capricious. But who's to say? That's only my envious perception and it may be skewed, as I'm no expert on their flight patterns. Because we tend to interpret everything in our own anthropocentric light, nature can appear abstruse, inconsistent. (Can anyone explain why a lion shakes her tail when she's angry and a dog when she is pleased?) We've stranded ourselves outside nature's canon of seeming contradictions and puzzles, and I've no doubt we miss out on a lot.

Around noon one midsummer's day, a pair of grey goshawks, with their blunt, broad wings slightly upswept, alternately glided, then ascended with quick wing beats, their pumping avian hearts, proportionally as much as four times larger than our human ones, beating eight times as fast.

Granted, I may not understand their states of mind, but I've lived in these parts long enough to appreciate that birds are pure poetry in motion and melody – literally as well as figuratively. Take, for example, trochee, the poetic metre comprising a long and then a short syllable. Now listen for it in the male whipbird's long explosive whipcrack followed by the female's 'choo-choo'. Or catch the eastern rosella at its undulating, long-long-short swoops of flight – palimbacchus. Or enjoy the laughing tribracchus rhythms of the firetails who hop – short-short-short. And the goshawks when they're gliding? Molossos – long, long long.

My destination was Scarabalotti's Lookout, a place whose vista is as honeyed as its name is mellifluous. From up there, the world posed still as a freeze-frame, although from Mother Nature I'd learned that a molecular maelstrom was always moving and seething just underneath this duplicitous snapshot.

Science confirms that a chair may not be solid. But that need not preclude my chintzing it with cabbage roses, sinking into its silky weave and draping my legs over its gently rounded arms. How much richer would our reality be if we remained aware of our complicity in this physical masquerade, this maya? How much more fun if we tinkered with the volume and frequency of our senses, those seductive dissemblers of beauty and truth? For in the evolving nature of personal reality, what is truth but a shifting shortwave?

Like a tiny brown bird perched on the long green arm of the ridge, I made a meal of the full-circle sweep – the opulent, rolling hinterland, the chequered coastal plain, the ocean as far as a glad eye could scan.

The concealed cloth of silence was all that covered and encoded the sumptuous spread, the shameless au naturel fandancing going on in every direction, and, I, lapping up the pellucid light in a dreamy mood, took my time to decide that for that afternoon on that day, colour was the only Rosetta

Stone[1] to watch out for. The landscape's beryl pigments[2] served no apparent evolutionary purpose – creation can be rash, extravagant – but then I wasn't scrutinising too closely, either. Einstein claimed that 'the longing to behold harmony' continued to be the main propellant of cosmology. But from that Olympian eyrie on that particular afternoon I was up for pure enchantment, not epiphany. Hence, through my own glazed viewfinder, I watched a tangerine hot air balloon trail the milky coastline as it sailed south through an ice blue expanse. The tinctures of earth, sea and sky blended effortlessly in an ambrosial elixir and I took a long, deep draught of its timelessness.

With apologies to Emily D, I offer the following corruption[3] of her ironic wisdom:

Nature concocts a splendid surfeit –
And Her menu's never too long;
'So instead of getting to heaven at last,
I'm going all along!'

Thoreau had a few canny things to say about being with and observing nature and from amongst the bones and beans[4] of his collected writings, I have picked out the eyes, to serve up (in the cannibalising tradition of so much writing) on these pages, a few that I regard as jewels. Here is one gem: 'Man cannot afford to be a naturalist, to look at nature directly, but only through the side of his eye. He must look through and beyond her.'

Perhaps Thoreau was right and a mere mortal may not look full upon a goddess and yet live. I mean, look what happened to Actaeon[5] when he accidentally saw Artemis at her midday bath.

And yet on that sublime Byron afternoon, unlike Pythagoras[6] and his recondite mathematical mob, I had no wish to avert my gaze from nature, from her fair or ferocious faces, her rabid, resounding rhythms, her endless, churning cycles of life-death-life. My lucky two[7] feet stood solidly on her red terrene and my spirit bowed in homage to Her in whom we all live and move and have our being.

This place, just like we locals, has its temperaments. Once, late at night in the middle of an electrical storm, a friend and I got the mad – or maybe not so mad – idea to go up to Scarabalotti's. On that wet, black evening, the silence rested naturally within him and me, while all around us the sound and light extravaganza crackled, boomed and flashed so spellbindingly that, we, identified with its wildness, could neither utter nor leave until it was all over.

But that gilded day the silence was suddenly broken by a fantasia of poignant trumpet notes. The player sat under a huge fig tree in an adjoining paddock, and his rendition of Charlie Chaplin's *Smile* was so sensitive and accomplished, I guessed he must be a professional. Around here, musos are as thick on the ground as paspalum, so there was a good chance this was the case. In the nutshell corral of country life, I did not have to wait long to find out. A couple of weeks later, I met the maestro, John Hoffman. He was a witty participant on a 'Creative Careers' panel for young people, which I chaired.

(Yes, Emily, I'm taking small doses of my own self-prescribed medicine and beginning to go out again.)

'How do you get started in the musical career of your choice?' one youth asked John.

'First you buy a fine musical instrument, an extremely expensive sound system and a whole batch of CD's you can't afford. That'll motivate you to get out and walk the streets for work,' John quipped, before offering some more pragmatic and less expensive suggestions.

*   *   *

Speaking of careers brings me to books and writing. Books are powerful entities. A certain book delved into at a particular time of life can move us, make us think, laugh, long, rejoice or recoil; it can lead us to change our occupations, outlooks, countries, lovers, life partners, or the lot.

Stephanie Dowrick once said: 'When a book is a great book for you, then it's a friend. And one of the ways in which it's a friend is that you can return to it when you need to. You can also talk about it to your friends.'

Here is the divine Miss D on the subject:

'There is no frigate like a book
To take us lands away,
Nor any coursers like a page
Of prancing poetry.
This traverse may the poorest take
Without oppress of toll;
How frugal is the chariot
That bears a human soul!'

In the days before I retreated fully into my own pink Paphos[8] to 'immure' myself 'and not be seen', I once interviewed on my program (*Between The Covers*, for local lovers of books and writing) on Bay-FM Community Radio a woman who had packed up and left the country in which she had been living and gone to a foreign shore to study with a much older woman whose spiritual journey and Sufi teachings she had read about in an autobiographical book[9]. The younger woman's boyfriend of that time was devastated to be ditched for a snowy-haired sage in her seventies.

One evening during the B.M.N. (Before Mother Nature) era when I was still trying to figure out exactly what it was I wanted to say and how I wanted to say it, and when, incidentally, I was wondering how I was going to pay my looming $280 phone bill, I casually plucked from one of my bookshelves a novel from which I wished to re-read a scorchingly witty scene which had, despite the passing years, remained vividly with me. I wanted to try to understand how the author had pulled off the hilarious literary hat trick that still had me smirking about it nearly a decade later. The book was Tom Wolfe's *The Bonfire of the Vanities*, which let rip on the 'vanities of high-life and low-life', the moneyed tribes, the wannabe's and the 'masters of the universe' of New York City during the 1980s – and my selecting it that night ended up saving my bacon.

The particular scene I was after had to be somewhere between the hardcovers (I'd bought the book in the 1980s when we were all on a big financial roll and could afford such luxuries). But where? It was a big book. By the time I got to page 503, I still hadn't found the scene. But I *had* found $260 in twenty dollar notes (the attractive, old-fashioned ones that felt like 'real' money). You never know your luck when scavenging amongst your own bookshelves.

Bonfire, appropriately enough, had been the chief hiding place for my spare cash in the days when I still had some. Those days now seemed to have happened in another lifetime and I'd forgotten all about my former cash stash system. Suddenly I wondered how much more aging currency I'd hidden in my other hardbacks, twelve boxes of which I'd sold at garage sales as part of a lighten-up-and-stay-solvent strategy.

Apart from being able to pay my phone bill, the other good thing about finding that money was that I saw it as a confirmatory sign that I was, indeed, heading in the right creative direction. (Writers can feel as fragile and insecure as any other artists in this regard.) For had I not wished to study Wolfe's technique, I would not have taken the book off the shelf.

Several seasons later, when I was halfway through writing this manuscript and in need of another kind of confirmation – that I was not barking up an Authorus ignoramus tree – I started the midnight fossicking routine again. And devoured a Matthew Fox book, *Original Blessing*.

Fox contends that 'everyone is a mystic or artist until our culture, religion or education drives this out of us.' *Original Blessing* empowers the reader and takes her or him back to their own creativity and that deep, ecstatic centre which resides beneath any fear of death. It is a hopeful book which guides us to rejoice and celebrate the uniqueness of our existence.

Fox sums up his spiritual framework as 'a bridge which carries us back to an ancient past and forward with hope to the future. It is also an umbrella under which the following persons can meet and share a common language: those dedicated to feminine wisdom, Earth and animal rights, renewed education, honouring the artists in us and around us, respect for the anawim[10] among us, global justice, mystical and religious renewal.'

And while we're on the subject of books and writers, I cannot miss this chink of opportunity to praise Shakespeare, who poured all of us into his great big theatrical melting pot of hopeful humanity and to this day, reminds us of the oneness of life; makes us realise, as Sybil Thorndike once said 'that we are all part and parcel of one another, and the joys and miseries of one are the joys and miseries of all ... and that is William Shakespeare's great contribution to us all and to our life in the world.'

Yet Shakespeare also retained the critical detachment essential to a good cook stirring the rich, dramatic broth of human nature. He knew that

'All the world's a stage,
And all the men and women merely players ...'

      *   *   *

When it comes to stages and players, messages and mediums, the tribal voices of writers, of course, are not the only ones being raised. During the drafting of the latter chapters, I participated in a protest rally (yes, Emily, going out again) where we, the local citizenry were sitting in a park watching the sun shine on one of the most beautiful views on this country's eastern seaboard, and trying to work out how to stop it from setting on a proposed four-lane freeway in the west.

The freeway would carve through the unspoiled scenic escarpment we love and cherish, and which is one of our main claims to international fame. Most of us around here enjoy the ambience of the country roads. We like to take our time, to take in the views. We regard the proposition of permanently speeding at 100ks as dangerous, insane.

At the rally, we were told that in order to stop the juggernaut of the Roads and Traffic Authority and to beat the big bucks and powerful lobbying of the transport industry; in order to protect our electorate, one of the most biodiverse in Australia, it was imperative that our fax machines keep transmitting to

Parliament House until they smoke (the machines, that is, not the Parliament, although the latter might not be such a bad idea).

Above the amplified rhetoric of the rally's speakers, a swoop of light and movement up high caught my attention. Eight ibis, those immaculate white skysailors, festooned the air, banking and turning in perfect formation. To which far shore or territory were they headed, I wondered, for ibis are known to travel spectacular distances. Birds banded north of Perth in Western Australia have shown up in the eastern states and in the Northern Territory. The ancient Egyptians, aware of the ibis' great assistance to agriculturists (the birds, voracious insect eaters, protect the crops) declared the bird sacred. Anyone who injured or killed an ibis was committing a crime and, by law, would be punished.

Amidst the day's depressing details of yet another impending crime 'against the biosphere', those ibis, for me, were a reminder of the priceless, life-preserving Polestar we're following. I refer, metaphorically, of course, to the brightest star in the constellation Ursa Minor and not to the American two-stage, intermediate-range ballistic missile, usually fired by a submerged submarine.

Tracking the ibis' lofty swerving, my thoughts took flight and settled for a while on the late Rachel Carson, the biologist and writer whose classic work *The Sea Around Us* spent eighty-six straight weeks on the *New York Times* best-seller lists and whose seminal work *Silent Spring* (which motivated governments in many countries to curb the use of pesticides) is debatably the most important book published this century. Recently I'd wanted to re-read *Spring*, but when I asked at the library soon after a documentary about Carson had screened on television, twenty 'holds' already had been placed on the three well-thumbed copies in circulation, so its power and influence still ripple across continents and through time. I conjected, presumptuously perhaps, that Carson would have delighted in a day such as this by the sea. Nature was her religion. She admitted: 'I am an idealist. I may never come to a full realisation of my dreams, but a man's reach must exceed his grasp or what's a heaven for.' That statement typified the reverence Rachel Carson had for life, even when she had to struggle against it (her lifelong health problems and, ultimately, the public attacks on her by the giant pesticide companies).

On the microphone, longtime local activist Annudhi Wentworth urged us to keep the letters rolling in to the powers-that-be: 'Don't let the motor car inherit the earth!' she implored. As she spoke, the keen-eyed amongst us sighted a frothy glimmer and two dark streaks of marine power in the distance – the spume-blowing and pec-waving of two humpbacks in the northern waters of the bay. The undiluted joy and irony of the timing of this second impromptu display had me shaking my head. Around here, life even manages to heap pulchritudes upon protest meetings. But for how long?

I cast my eye around to check out the tribe who had turned up. I saw hundreds of people I knew. I saw a tribe that went way beyond any radical green fringe. I saw that we were young and old; we were businessmen and businesswomen; we were doctors and lawyers; we were high school students and academics; we were farmers and healers and musicians and artists and hairdressers and singers and nurses. We were builders and bakers and – Byron being a hive of diverse and alternative activity – documentary and candlestick makers. We were people from the coast and people from the hills. We were a noisy, opinionated, highly politicised tribe. We had

240

already won a few landmark environmental cases. And we were braced for more to come.

We know that our unspoiled landscape and our friendly, small-town atmosphere are our greatest assets. We want to fatten up the goose that laid the golden egg, not kill it. We value our simple lifestyles and strong sense of community. We are willing to rock the pillars of today's prevailing but perilously impermanent worldview – economic rationalism and the material cult of more, bigger, better, ad infinitum. We want to pass on a life-sustaining biosphere to our children and grandchildren. We want to give something back to a planet on which places like this are increasingly rare. In all this, we, naturally, are not alone. We are a microcosm for what is happening all over Australia, all over the globe.

People are painting and sculpting, writing and photo-graphing, teaching and tending, dancing and singing, meditating, chanting, visualising, healing the sick in body and spirit, caring for the creatures, praying and walking the land – celebrating, praising and reciprocating in a thousand different ways the unconditional amplitude the Earth extends to us. Still others are planting trees, repairing the land, growing their own vegetables. Some show up one day a year to Clean Up Australia. Some are writing letters to governments, some are donating to local action groups or fund-raising for them. Some are contacting the media and girding their loins for major battles and minor skirmishes too numerous to name. Every second, everywhere, people are awakening to the moss-velvet blessing that the Universe has rained down upon us. They are lifting their consciousness from the quicksands of fear and the 'limitations' trumpeted by social consciousness, and daring to dream the Earth-honouring dreams of their ancestors; they are finding new ways to create, to renew, to care, share and heal, to perpetuate the heart-opening heritage of this divine and delicate planet which, through the darkness and light of desecration and consecration, through disaster and deliverance, belongs to us as we belong to her. Sun-seeking grassroots are hardy, rampant and will thrust themselves up even through the concrete centres of cities.

Cynics may say we are just an international mob of Nimby's[11], but I see all the hearts of our global clan linked up by something bigger than that. From within and without, we have seen the light, and wherever we are on the planet, each one of us is a point of it. We have heard the wild, green voices calling 'each to each' and we are calling back. We are the voices of the Earth. And we are one helluva big tribe.

At the close of the anti-freeway rally, under a huge Norfolk pine, my friends and I said our farewells. They were going to collect their children from ballet practice. I was off to choir rehearsal (yes, Emily, going out again). As I walked off, I found myself humming a familiar tune. The lyrics momentarily eluded me, but something about the melody heartened me. Then I remembered its context and traced the fount of my optimism. Yothu Yindi[12] once gave an outdoor concert here which, for me, endures as one of those incomparably bewitching Byron evenings. Only a few of their words came back to me then, but they were enough:

'Don't be afraid of the move you make
You better listen to your tribal voice.'

1. An ancient Egyptian stone bearing inscriptions the decipherment of which led to the understanding of hieroglyphic writing. By examining the direction in which the bird and animal characters faced, Thomas Young of England also discovered the way in which hieroglyphic signs were to be read.
2. According to Rachel Carson in *The Sea Around Us*: 'The sea is blue

because the sunlight is reflected back to our eyes from the water molecules or from very minute particles suspended in the sea.' The landscape is green because the green pigment in plants traps the energy of sunlight for photosynthesis and exists in several forms, the most abundant being chlorophyll. It is also used as a colouring agent in medicine or food. The sky is the apparently dome-shaped expanse extending upwards from the horizon, which (because of the scattering of light rays) is characteristically blue or grey during the day, red in the evening and black at night.

3. Dickinson's original poem, *A Service of Song*, stanza three, read:
'God preaches, – a noted clergyman, –
And the sermon is never long;
So instead of getting to heaven at last,
I'm going all along.'

4. Thoreau grew his own beans. See footnote in Chapter 14.

5. Artemis, the virgin (Greek) goddess of the hunt and the moon, turned the hunter, Actaeon into a stag after he saw her in her full glory bathing in a hidden pool at noon. He fled, but was ripped to pieces by his own hounds.

6. Greek philosopher and mathematician Pythagoras of Samos founded a religious, secrecy-bound brotherhood which followed a life of strict asceticism and greatly influenced the development of mathematics and its application to music and astronomy, and the science of modern physics. Pythagoreans, according to Margaret Wertheim in *Pythagoras' Trousers* (see recommended reading) aimed to escape from nature. This transcendence, says Wertheim, 'also implied transcending "the feminine" because in Pythagoreanism, as in most Greek thought, matter – the very substance of nature – was considered inherently female'.

7. Wertheim (see footnote 6) writes: 'In Pythagorean cosmology, the number two was not only the supreme female principle, but also the number associated with matter. Meanwhile, the supreme male principle, the number one, was equated directly with the supreme immaterial deity, Apollo.' Wertheim explains that odd numbers were considered male and even ones female; the Pythagoreans regarded the odd ones as 'good' and the even ones as 'evil'.

8. A village in southwest Cyprus, near the sites of two ancient cities: famous as the centre of Aphrodite worship and traditionally the place at which she landed after her birth among the waves.

9. *Daughter of Fire: A Diary of a Spiritual Training with a Sufi Master*, by Irina Tweedie. Published by The Golden Sufi Centre, Inverness, California, 1986.

10. In *The Coming of the Cosmic Christ* (see recommended reading), Fox defines the anawim as 'the little and forgotten ones, the oppressed victims of social justice'.

11. An acronym for Not In My Back Yard.

12. The Yothu Yindi band members are Yolngu people who hail from the coastal communities of Arnhem Land's Gove Peninsula.

28

Reflections

Going down to my local beach always reminds me of being born. I've been cocooned, writing for ages on the 'inside', when suddenly I hear the roar of the breaking waters, the contractions begin and the big push to get out into the wider world is on. The birth canal is the path cut through the big entrance dune, which I enter through a shady tunnel of tuckeroo trees. I emerge on the 'outside', wide-eyed, wet, salty or licked alive by the wind, reborn into any one of myriad scenarios, for this beach, like all beaches, has its moods, its changing casts and hues.

These alter, subtly or dramatically, from hour to hour, from moment to moment. If I come down morning, noon and dusk on the same day, I can be gobsmacked by the awesome manifoldness of creation. I may find myself invigorated by an early splash in a choppy, overcast Pacific, burnished by midday's merciless rays, then swaddled in sunset's rubescence. When I can retain the raw receptivity of infancy, the innocent eye of childhood, these are votive scenes. They're precious gifts and just the jolt to get me breathing deeply.

Cresting the dune one autumn morning, I crane my neck

for a quick preview. A long clean streak of space, it's unpeopled, for the Easter break is over and the tourists have departed, but it is far from a subdued natal setting. It is all airy animation and effulgence down here. The sky is a glistening jellyfish blue (some jellyfish actually manufacture their own light); the light is crystalline, flowing down onto the beach in a white confluence. The salty, sybaritic smell of freedom, like a heat-seeking emission, flies straight up my nostrils.

A lenient sou'easter has the clouds doing some stunning shapeshifting. Overhead, the cumulus have pearly white crowns and distended underbellies of pale taupe. Down at Broken Head, they're draping whole ravines in dark nebulae. Up towards the Cape they are pure ivory, backlit, trailing diffuse streamers of light. Banked in holy masses, they look like religious postcards drifting towards Queensland. This sky, like every sky, like a fingerprint, is unique. *The clouds the clouds the clouds* I say, a reflexive daily mantra. The cumulonimbus out to sea are storeys high, their slate foundations fat with rain and hung low enough to graze the horizon.

I look and look at that blurry hyacinth line which the dictionary calls 'the range or limit of scope, interest, knowledge'. For a short while, I project my thoughts beyond it, directly – give or take a few islands – to Chile. The Chileans, I assume, revere their land and seascapes, too. There must be literature, art, to attest. Some other time I might ask at the library; right now I'm up to my limit on the borrowing quota.

In a library book, I once happened upon an extract from Charles Lyell's *Principles of Geology* (1830-3) which said: 'We know that one earthquake may raise the coast of Chile for a hundred miles to an average height of about five feet. A repetition of two thousand shocks of equal violence might produce a mountain chain one hundred miles long and ten thousand feet high. Now should ... one of these conclusions happen in a century, it would be consistent with the order of events experienced by the Chileans from the earliest times.' That made the survival tactics of Mother Nature and the Chileans sound pretty impressive. But Chile is a momentary idyll. The true, magnetic compass of my interest is *here*, latitude 28:41,longtitude 153:37, and *now*, 11am-ish (I don't wear a watch anymore).

Most natural landscapes, even those which superficially appear barren or bland, are, I believe, rich, multilayered and idiosyncratic. Initially, their surface lines present a pattern of immediately obvious attractions and deficiencies. But since most of them have survived colorful histories that are longer than we can comfortably comprehend, they may also harbour less apparent qualities – such as antediluvian wisdom, ingrained contradictions, unalloyed compassion, buried vulnerabilities. They may hum with hidden powers and stream with serpentine stories, dark mysteries, magic, myths, poetry and parables. They may cradle deep energies from which may flow either or both of the twin tributaries of delight and tribulation.

These interred treasures cannot instantly be detected or grabbed at by the greedy or the casually curious. Rather, it seems, *they* may unfold themselves, their portents, promises and higher purposes when we are in the right frame of mind. My own (adult) receptivity to these disclosures developed very subtly, very gradually right here in my own locale. My experience is that place is an active force, capable of a cogent interaction with us, capable of carving a deeply meaningful intaglio in our hearts.

I think about this place, my home, and how it has seduced

me, for better or worse, for richer or poorer, into marrying the Muse; how it has enticed me to put down roots in Joseph Campbell country – following my bliss, trusting the garden path of organic creativity to lead me through some fresh green fields along the way. Dare I dream of publication, a process which allows others to travel, through the apertures of their imaginations, to the places I have been and to conjure up their versions of the wonders I have seen? This writing, sprawling as it does, across different literary territories, and colored as it is with affirmation, awe, hope ('the thing with feathers/That perches in the soul,/ and sings the tune without the words'), celebration and gratitude amid a media-managed world of cynicism and negativity, may not find a marketplace niche, let alone have a long and fruitful shelflife. And if that's how the copy crumbles, then 'it wasn't meant to be', as we tend to say around here. Still, publication or no, during this, my own organically home-grown 'Course in Miracles' and 'Creation Time', I have gained some priceless experience and understanding.

If – and there is 'much virtue in If' – for just a microsecond, I allow myself to be enlightened, I can feel in my bones that, finally, it does not matter where 'time' takes me, or any of us. One day – who knows? – I may check out of this coastal coven. Somewhere, sometime, I'm bound to say my fond farewells to the flexings and fumings of the whole restless planet. But on another plane, I remain convinced that a part of me has been abducted and bound (but not gagged) by the spirit of this place. And surely it was that spirit which, in the dawn of consciousness and in this morning's sunrise, found itself roused by the desire of intent and dreamed itself into physical existence. So in every moment the hills and valleys, waters and woods are formed anew, freshly energised with the magnetic creativity of their timeless source. A place, a plane – a *home* – thus Infinitely pervaded, compels.

* * *

My friend Susie Shepherd, who lived for several years in this district, and who, due to my 'wise taciturnity', knew nothing of the subject matter of this book, wrote to me of her recent experience at the intricately eroded badlands from Zabriskie Point in Death Valley, California. 'When I arrived, I knew that the land and I needed to communicate – how pretentious that sounds! So I sat on the top of the lookout and just gave myself over. The silence was so deep and profound that the land insisted you lose your head noise and just be. I felt cleansed by the whole experience (and still do when I bring that rare afternoon back) and fell deeply in love with the whole area – strange for a coastal girl!'

Have we not always projected on to the landscape and extracted from it the impressions and insights we require for comfort, meaning, or a wake-up call in our lives and times? Have we not always doused it with our presumptions, conceptions, our dreams and anthropocentric designs? The trouble with treating the landscape as a spiritual analogue is that we run the risk of missing its inherent message or mythic imprint and ending up in an echoing canyon of tropes, a mudslide of metaphor. In tribal cultures and in Eastern spirituality, myths are still perceived literally and enacted ritually by people. We Westerners, in our urbanised, increasingly uniform lifestyles, long ago lost our edgeless blending, our identification with mythic reality. If we ever stop to consider it at all, we hold it, fascinated, at academic or poetic arm's length or we relax in our armchairs, watching documentaries about it on that 'universal mandala', the television set.

Still, metaphor has its role to play, inspiring or guiding us, as it marries mystery and meaning in potent and poetic forms. Indeed, metaphor may not be such a lost cause since, as Barry Lopez has written: 'To inquire into the intricacies of a distant landscape, then, is to provoke thoughts about one's interior landscape, and the familiar landscapes of memory. The land urges us to come around to an understanding of ourselves.' Loren Eiseley put it like this: 'It is ours to transmute, not iron, not copper, not gold, but our tracks through nature, to see them finally attended by self-knowledge . . .'

Such knowledge, it strikes me, often evolves in tandem with a rise in green consciousness, an awareness that, as Paul Devereux says 'if we are the disease, then the healing of that ill is the way to save the Earth's environment as we need it to be'. Yes, we should keep on recycling, replanting, repairing, reducing consumption. Indeed we should escalate our efforts in those directions. But what needs healing as much as the planet is our relationship to her, and that can only take place through a quantum leap in our consciousness. Peter Marshall claims: 'Ecological thinking is rising in human minds like sap in spring. What is taking place is not merely a concern with cleaning up our environment but a fundamental shift in consciousness – as momentous as the Renaissance.'

There are optimistic signs that this shift *is* underway and these should be brought to mind, especially when so many of us despair at the colossal effort ahead of us to create a sustainable way of living on planet Earth. While pledging constant vigilance, we should also remind ourselves of how far we've already come. Not more than a generation back, most Australians had never heard of the ozone layer, global warming, acid rain or the Gaia hypothesis. Nowadays, thanks to environmentalists slogging and slanging it out in all levels of the social and political hierarchy (from the highest governments' offices to local community action groups), most of us are au fait with terms like 'environmental impact statement', 'endangered species', 'ecology'. Australia, according to Judith Wright has 'one of the most active and well-informed conservation movements in the world'.

*   *   *

Straight ahead a couple is fishing. She has just caught something. A white flash flails desperately on the sand until she smothers it with a weighted covering. I am a fish-eater. I avert my eyes, and thank that creature for its life. The fishers have picked a good spot. Half a dozen gannets circle overhead and suddenly one dives so ferociously, so ... *vertiginously*, it must surely smash itself on the aquamarine below. But no. Although a diving gannet hits the water at ninety-six kilometres per hour, this plunge was, as usual, aerodynamically perfect. It is hard to tell if the bird has caught something because gannets seize fish in their serrated bills and often swallow them before surfacing. In any event, it rises effortlessly from the wash. This dazzling routine is one I've seen often, yet each time it affects me the same way. My feet take root like a mangrove in the wet shore and I bear a marvelling kind of witness to the sheer risk and dare of that life-supporting manoeuvre. Of course, the gannets, who need neither affectation nor applause to get them through their days, are not being grandiloquent. It's all just breakfast, lunch and dinner to them. Or is it? Blind instinct, you might say. Or, watching all those perspicacious encores, you might perceive that the gannets' airborne artistry is so effortlessly

250

and immaculately blended into their lives that the two are inseparable. Who am I, grappling to express and assimilate my own creativity into my life, to deny them that brilliant merger?

A swift scan of the sky reveals no sign of a brahminy kite, but a wedge-tailed shearwater is dynamically soaring on the prevailing winds. Suddenly it parachutes with its wings spread to the max. Devilishly it dips, catches another updraft and soars statically (its tail feathers fanned out and flapping furiously), before gliding, then dropping, then beating the force of gravity at its own game one more time, and lifting higher and higher. Is it scouting for food or is it trying to get somewhere? Is it testing the wind direction or is it – here's that curly one again – just having fun? On a scintillating, red-letter day like today, wouldn't you?

The tide is way out, the sand still moist from the previous night's rain and the ocean has sculpted afresh the long bleached shoreline to the south. I start towards Broken Head, paddling in the shallows. A young kelpie up ahead runs widdershins around the clear, kidney-shaped lagoon that wasn't there yesterday, chasing a white-faced heron, scattering the silver gulls who've gathered on its seaward bar. I wonder how old they are, for I've heard that gulls, aside from being masters of thermodynamics, can live for as long as thirty years. They lift off, soar in a streamlined circle for a few minutes, then descend like a deluge of white teardrops, their harsh, plaintive cries tempering a sanguine sky which, this morning is giving the turquoise waters a run for their money in the universal beauty stakes. Or seen in another light, the ethers and the ocean are not competitors at all, but a smooth double act, moving and gliding in a curvy dance of their own devising. However you view things, it's quite a scene down here. My bare feet trip lightly along the shore. I step out in a chest-filling faith that a grand choreographer is at work.

Curves, I think. Curves. The whole universe, all of our lives, seem comprised of them. Given enough travelling time, they will fulfill themselves into circles, cycles. No mathematician am I, but it appears to me that depending on the angle of the curve incurred at the outset and the speed at which its trajectory is travelled, the circle described could take a minute or a million millennium, or longer, to complete itself. Before the latter timeline, the mind virtually halts, while Nature abides and advances, intentional, unrushed, relentless. She certainly puts this life cycle of mine into perspective – barely a blink in the eye of the Eternal. Is it purposeful or is it punitive? Is it a palliative or a reprieve? Does it offer pleasures? Or is it just a bitter pill? The perceptual choice in every moment is mine.

The climate of a locality, according to the Australian Bureau of Meteorology, is 'the synthesis of day-to-day values of the meteorological elements that affect the locality. Synthesis here implies more than simple averaging. Climatic data are usually expressed in terms of an individual calendar month or season and are determined over a period (usually about thirty years) long enough to ensure that representative values for the month or season are obtained.' Thirty years strikes me as long cycle.

Cycles, I think. Cycles. The lives of my sisters flash before me and, as is sometimes my wont, I lapse into headline-precis, a hangover from all those years of writing for tabloids and broadsheets. The poster banners read: MOTHER OF THREE TURNS MINI-MOGUL and WHIRLING DERVISH DECIDES TO RECONSTRUCT. And my own – CAREER GIRL GOES GODDESS. I laugh . . .

It's hard to be a post-modernist in paradise, even one that's giving itself a slow, lingering kiss goodbye.

*   *   *

On the return stretch north on my beach walk, I go as far as the beach entrance signed 10B. A small group of sacred kingfishers has been nesting in the upper part of the sandbank nearby and I am always hoping to glimpse them. In the soft sand, I sit motionless and wait, wondering what kind of attachment, if any, those green-black-and-buff-tinged birds have to this place. Perhaps they live in a kind of Zen reality in which they've cut the Cupid's string of attachment to place. The phrase 'free as a bird' obviously is derived from some-where. It strikes me that, as avian addresses go, 10B Tallow Beach, Byron Bay, Australia, 2481, is as dandy a one as a bird could wish for. If birds could wish, that is. Which, of course, like most creatures, they cannot. So we tend to do it for them. Anthropomorphism has its sunny side, too. The kingfishers clearly are not in residence at this hour, so I stroll on.

Just inside the breakers a large black patch of something catches my eye. Perhaps it is a rock recently uncovered. That seems unlikely, although the local surfers will tell you: the rips and undertows are violent and unpredictable 'round here. Yesterday's valleys and troughs are today's hidden sandbars, and you can come a cropper if you don't watch out. I look and look into that chameleon element, trying to decipher its lambent legerdemain.

The dark shape draws me into its languid roll and thrall, until my gaze grows filmy with ... what? Reflection? It's hard to say, for my mind is cast adrift from critical perception, from the need to assign meaning or to adduce. Time is unhinged and I feel myself carried somehow out and down to an expansive perceptibility beyond that of ordinary recounting, to a level far beneath the froth of incident and detail. Deep in this unseen current, the light still penetrates, yet all distinction between animate and inanimate, matter and spirit, dissolves. Everything is alight with vibrating energy. Even the most beguiling play of words cannot recreate that wavelength, but like all waves, it rolls in and eventually breaks. When it does, and 'normal' sensory cognition returns, I finally settle on an ambiguous determination. The patch could be a submerged pod of dolphins or a large inky mantle of seaweed sailing south, I decide, but keep a close eye on it, anyway.

Yes, it's an engaging spectacle down here, flowing and ebbing and pulsing with aliveness. I can't even begin to envisage the whole multitudinous company responsible for today's cosmorama (the insects, the pollinators, the parasites, the bacteria, the microbes, the soil builders, the teeming life in the shifting sea, the slant of the wind – no less important for being small or invisible). Never the same show twice. Today the backstage cues from Mother Nature are that all of us in this long, long-running hit production have been loved unconditionally a priori. This, she assures me, is an apodictic truth.

All at once I feel like a siphon through which gratitude is torrenting. Inside the moving vessel of my body, the pressure of this grace dams up until I am brim-full, bulging to bursting point. My stoicism is up against my sensitive side. The battle of the Titans rages for several more strides and then the siphon cracks and I am awash in the spillway of my own salty thankfulness.

*　*　*

But in many places now, the Earth is scarred, sick or eerily silent (the nearest example to me is a massive quarry whose ghostly gouged moonscape gives me a visceral stab). Amid the fast, fractious clamour of our lifestyles, we rarely notice her wounding or silence. And when we are reminded, usually by the media in its formularised, data-based, A-versus-B reportage, its facile seven-second grabs, we feel so guilty and overwhelmed by the life-threatening statistics of death and destruction, it's easier to switch off and turn our attention elsewhere.

Theodore Roszak says that reason alone, the ecological facts and figures of the frontline environmentalists, cannot shame or scare us into the psychological transformation that is essential for real change to occur. I'm with him. Surely we need not only to recognise for whom the bell tolls, but to feel the mighty power of its poignant reverberations, its lamentation of loss in our own beings. Yet while we heed the bell, we also need to keep singing our own songs of praise and love for the Earth, for the stupendous mystery of existence we share with her, for the cosmic blessing of being here now.

Ultimately, Peter Marshall counters, 'nature is neither male nor female; it is both, a complex, mysterious, multifaceted unity.' He warns that assigning 'gender or status to gods and goddesses is a form of idolatory; it separates spirits from nature as free-floating particles, and places them in a transcendental pantheon of human values'.

Maybe.

But, it's almost impossible not to think in terms of metaphors, images and analogies. Earthbound still, and branded male and female by our bodies, if not our psyches, we are nothing if not beautiful birds of paradox and polarity, hungrily picking from the tree of life the sweetest, most nourishing seeds of archetypal and dualistic truth.

Rupert Sheldrake hits the mark by noting that 'our conception of nature is intertwined with ideas about the relations between women and men, between goddesses and gods, and between the feminine and the masculine in general. If we prefer to reject these traditional sexual associations, what are the alternatives to the idea of nature as organic, alive and motherlike? One is that nature consists of nothing but inanimate matter in motion. But in this case we only deny the mother principle by being unaware of it; the very word for matter is derived from the same root as *mother* – in Latin, the corresponding words are *materia* and *mater* – and the whole ethos of materialism is permeated with maternal metaphors.'

Rather than trying to transcend these gender associations, we could try to acknowledge, honour and respect the differences between our inner masculine and feminine – each creates benefits and drawbacks – and to integrate and express them in ever-adjusting balance.

Right now, the planetary scales are weighed down by the masculine principle – and humanity and nature are paying dearly for the imbalance. Everywhere you look, there are fearful automatons, working without thinking, consuming without conscience, acting without awareness. Productivity, that hell-for-leather Prince of Darkness, has benighted our vision.

To tilt the scales back to equilibrium, we need to weigh in with a substantial dose of the feminine principle in our lives. Art, music, meditation, poetry, surfing, bushwalking, digging in the dirt or whatever form of connection to the living universe takes our fancy will help to ignite understanding, inject optimism, catalyse creativity and restore balance. Not least of all we need to allow ourselves time to 'be,' rather than to 'do'; to exult in the vitality and validity of our sheer beingness. If that seems an alien or unlikely concept, it only goes to show how far out of kilter we've careened.

My card-carrying crusader days are behind me, and though my personal patina develops a deeper shade of green as time goes by, I am no seaside sibyl or sophist. I am a writer and, like Judith Wright, I remain obstinately a writer. 'Writers,' as she notes, 'are authorities on nothing.' But for what it's worth, here's my take on the way things stand.

We have forsaken the sanctity of Nature and we are rapidly losing the lingua franca that provides mutual understanding and cooperation between Her and us. That language is essentially the mythic, the contemplative, the artistic, the poetic. Nature is our mother, not our adversary or slave, and we need to learn to nurture Her and be nurtured by Her, not to conquer or exploit Her.

Amen. And to do this, you start –

– with yourself.

Exactly. Each individual's efforts increase the potentiality of all that is. So this puts a big responsibility upon every consciousness. As the slogan says –

The personal *is* the political?

You got it!

A pleasant expansion permeated my being. My physical boundaries s-t-r-e-t-c-h-e-d to accommodate a tremendous flow of energy. Like a singer at one with the music, I felt the song was inside me, and simultaneously I was inside the song. I couldn't tell whether it was me or Mother Nature gently calling us all to task.

It's both of us, working together. You conjure me up as a conduit of universal wisdom and creativity. I count on your cast of mind for this cooperative shifting of energy through the ethers.

It's not so extraordinary, really. I mean, aren't you earthlings overdue to mend your delusional divisions in the larger sum of yourselves? Each of you is familiar with the one who moves and manoeuvres and does, but few of you tune in to the one who breathes and dreams and knows how to simply be. For this reason, few of you have experienced non-action as a way to create your reality. Yet these inner aspects are neither dead nor irretrievably lost to you, just poleaxed by your cultural conditioning.

Spending time in my domain will help you to become aware of your inner senses and to dilute some of the duality which, in your sphere, makes you feel alienated. As you re-establish your relationship to the natural world, you will (if you'll excuse the pun) quite naturally start to behave, individually and collectively, locally and globally, as if the holy essence in every molecule mattered.

The onslaught of 'progress' is relentless and we must be indefatigable in our efforts (whatever form they may take) to heal our conterminal worlds – the masculine outer world obviously, but more critically at this time in our planetary evolution, the feminine inner. Only our assiduous and balanced attention to both realms will ultimately make a real difference to life on Earth.

Asked where his hope for the future lies, Thomas Berry replies that it 'rests extensively on the new vigour, assertion, and acceptance of women, especially their quality of nurturance. It is quite true that nurturance is not the only context in which women function, but I consider the future lies in the nurturing role because it is a primary role for all things in relationship to one another. Nurturance is also a primary, if presently underdeveloped quality of men. My hope that this change will take place springs from the fact that the new context of the human is being participated in so extensively by women. Fortunately we now have women in the law schools, the medical profession, religious seminaries, all branches of professional training, as well as the ecological movement.'

In Berry's view, our relationship with the natural world is not simply another moral problem, it is 'a profoundly *religious* problem'. What the westernised world needs, he says, is a creative dream, a vision. 'What is causing the difficulty at the present time is a destructive dream. The industrial age is driven by this illusory Wonderworld dream. In reality, though, we awaken, not to Wonderworld, but to ''Wasteworld''.'

As for what lies ahead, Berry notes 'the ''future'' is already happening. The movement is already in position; whether nor not we will carry it through is up to us.'

What to *do*? That characteristic question of our modern, mechanistic minds rears its badgering head yet again. To answer, I borrow firstly from Byron: 'A drop of ink may make a million think,' and then from Tennyson: 'More things are wrought by prayer than this world dreams of.' And then I stop my pacing and recline on the damp sand so delicately depressed by the swirling trails of pipis. I close my eyes, my eyes who've seen the glory of the annals of life – of where we've been, where we are and where we're going – written in rock, river, feather and bark, in lightning, sunsets and starry, starry nights, in every petal and leaf in this cardinal point of our old island continent. I breathe deeply and wait for Mother Nature to come through:

———————————

My Dear Child,

Your fellow scribe Tennyson was right. You cannot begin to imagine how much happens for the individual and collective good each time you go into the stillness, into silent communion with the subtle realms. And so I would like to give you another meditation to work with.

Allow yourself to visualise in your belly button a tiny sideways turquoise eight or infinity sign. As you watch that infinity sign in your belly button, you begin to notice that it is moving turquoise light. And as you breathe into it, you begin to feel that you are breathing in gold light through your mouth and your nose, and it's moving down, down into the centre of your belly button. And as the gold light gets there, the turquoise eight is getting larger and larger. Allow yourself to see this turquoise light getting larger and larger, the more breath you take. Now allow yourself to see this turquoise light expanding until it is as wide as the Earth is. You see that one

side of the turquoise eight is on one side of the Earth
and the other is on the other side of the Earth and the
point in the middle is inside your belly button. And
you are suspended in the very middle of the Earth.
And as you are suspended there, you are able to see
and perceive her heartbeat. You are able to see and
perceive her depth. You are able to see and perceive
her beauty.

Now allow yourself to feel your right hand
stretching out to the side of the Earth and your left
hand stretching out to the side of the Earth – so that
your hands are now stretched out as big as the Earth
is. And simply say: 'Use me Mother. Use these hands.
Use my throat. Use my mind.'

Breathing deeply. Use this meditation to remind
yourself of your purpose. And as you finish your
meditation, see the little infinity sign coming all the
way back to the centre of your belly button. It is
always there.

And I am always here for you to call upon.

With love and light,

Mother Nature.

P.S. Oh, and one farewell blessing: May the metaphors be with you!

*　　*　　*

I open my eyes and walk on my way again, casually keeping
tabs on the mystery floater. As someone still learning the art
of going with life's tides, I envy its effortless coasting and
say So Be It!

I breathe in the pristine air of privilege to be here in this palladium of gems, even though I'm shuffling my feet in the sand, trying to find my own rhythm, to learn my small part in this never-ending musical of the spheres. I count my riches piling up in the quality of my life (rather than in my standard of living) – in the luxury of time for quietude and reflection, in the mass of terra incognita that keeps me wondering, and the fabulous feast of beauty that satisfies the most famished or gluttonous eyes, those portals to other principalities. Living here, my heart is unapologetically on my sleeve a lot of the time. Yothu Yindi's music is on my brain again. 'This is my kind of life,' I'm humming. My kind of life.

That a significant slice of my recent past has been swallowed up by talking to birds and trees, to land and sea, moon and stars, to dead cats, dead poets, to thin air and broad daylight, may, I am aware, come across to some people as a little odd. By way of explanation, all I can say is that the heart and soul put no parameters on time; neither do they circumscribe communing or orisons to other worlds, and that in the process of Mother Nature's communiqués, I've been fathoming more than I ever dreamed possible. A few things I've twigged to are: that during the course of these great and grand cycles of life we all pass through, true nourishment comes from sources more mysterious and ethereal than fancy food stores and trendy tapas bars; that a perfect order reigns throughout all the elements of nature, and that we humans, as natural beings, are inherently divine members of that wondrous order.

I pick up a stick and hurl it as close to the shady drifter as I can. Sauntering south, I continue my ruminations: Is it simply a seaweed blanket, or is it something else? Is it a living organism, a sentient fleck in the field of infinite creativity? What essential part does it play in this complex mosaic? And then I stop short. What compels us to collect every drop of minutiae into our cloud of knowing? Must we relentlessly classify and define? Must we penetrate even the most minor mysteries?

Wordsworth said: 'We murder to dissect.' And Rilke reckoned we should: '... try to love *the questions themselves* as if they were locked rooms or books written in a very foreign language ... *Live* the questions now. Perhaps then, someday far in the future, you will gradually, without even noticing it, live your way into the answer.'

Turning homewards, I desist from further investigations into the 'morphology of the amorphous'. Amidst the carnival of words, one can try to whittle things down, to hint at the will-o'-the-wisp, but some things, ultimately, thankfully, remain unsayable. Instead, I sniff the moment in a puff of breeze and let all the big questions rest in my mind, trusting that Mother Nature has etched the answers lovingly, indelibly on my heart, and that these will flow through the dark veins of all my bright days.

Recommended Reading

Altman, Nathaniel *Sacred Trees*, Sierra Club Books, San Francisco, 1994

Anderson, Sherry Ruth and Patricia Hopkins *The Feminine Face of God: The Unfolding of the Sacred in Women*, Bantam Books, USA, 1992

Berry, Thomas *The Dream of the Earth*, A Sierra Club Book, San Francisco, 1988

——*Befriending the Earth: A Theology of Reconciliation between Humans and the Earth*, Twenty Third Publications, Mystic, Connecticut, 1995

Bolen Shinoda, Jean *Goddesses In Every Woman: A New Psychology of Women*, Harper Collins, New York, 1985

Campbell, Joseph *The Hero With a Thousand Faces*, Princeton University Press, Princeton, New Jersey, 1968

Campbell, Joseph with Bill Moyers *The Power of Myth*, Doubleday, New York, 1988

Campbell, Joseph *Myths To Live By*, Souvenir Press, London, 1973

Campbell, Joseph, with Fraser Boa *The Way of Myth*, Shambhala, Boston, 1994

Carey, John, editor *The Faber Book of Science*, Faber and Faber, London, 1995

Carson, Rachel *Silent Spring*, Hamilton, London, 1963

——*The Sea Around Us*, Staples Press, London, 1953

Chatwin, Bruce *Songlines*, Picador in association with Jonathan Cape, 1987

Devereux, Paul *Revisioning the Earth: A Guide to Opening the Healing Channels, Mind and Body*, Simon and Schuster, New York, 1996

Dickinson, Emily *The Works of Emily Dickinson*, Wordsworth Editions Ltd, UK, 1994

Dillard, Annie *Pilgrim at Tinker Creek*, Perennial Classics, Harper and Row, USA, 1996

Eiseley, Loren *The Star Thrower*, Harcourt Brace Jovanovich, New York, 1978

Emerson, Ralph Waldo *On Nature*, Shambhala, Boston, London, 1994

Findhorn Community *The Findhorn Garden*, Findhorn Press, Turnstone Books and Wildwood House, Great Britain, 1988

Fox, Matthew *Original Blessing: A Primer in Creation Spirituality*, Bear and Co, Santa Fe, New Mexico, 1983

——*The Coming of the Cosmic Christ: The Healing of Mother Earth and the Birth of a Global Renaissance*, Harper and Row, San Francisco, 1988

Fox, Matthew and Rupert Sheldrake *Natural Grace: Dialogues on Creation, Darkness, and The Soul in Spirituality and Science*, Doubleday, New York, 1996

Fraser, Sir James George *The Golden Bough: A Study in Magic and Religion*, (See especially 'Tree Worship'), Simon and Schuster, 1996

Griffin, Susan *Woman and Nature: The Roaring Inside Her*, Perennial Library, Harper and Row, USA, 1980

Hyde, Lewis *The Gift: Imagination and The Erotic Life of Property*, Vintage Books, Random House, New York, 1983

Jordan, William *Divorce Among the Gulls: An Uncommon Look at Human Nature*, Abacus, Little Brown and Company, London, 1991

Kellaway, Deborah, editor *The Virago Book of Women Gardeners*, Virago, London, 1996

Kooyman, Rob *Growing Rainforest*, State Forests of New South Wales, Casino district, Australia, 1996

Lopez, Barry *Arctic Dreams: Imagination and Desire in a Northern Landscape*, Picador (Pan Books), London, 1987

Lorenz, Konrad *King Solomon's Ring: New Light on Animal Ways*, Crowell, New York, 1952

Marshall, Peter *Nature's Web: Exploration of Ecological Thinking*, Simon and Schuster, London, 1992

Maxwell, Gavin *Ring of Bright Water*, Pan Books, London, 1963

Neihardt, John G. *Black Elk Speaks: Being the Life Story of a Holy Man of the Oglala Sioux*, Pocket Books, New York, 1972

Paglia, Camille *Sexual Personae: Art and Decadence from Nefertiti to Emily Dickinson*, Yale University Press, New Haven, 1990

Pizzey, Graham and Frank Knight *A Field Guide to the Birds of Australia*, Angus and Robertson, Australia, 1997

Pollard, Michael *Second Nature: A Gardener's Education*, Bloomsbury, London, 1996

Rawlence, Christopher, editor *About Time*, Jonathan Cape, London, 1985

Roberts, Elizabeth and Elias Amidon *Earth Prayers from Around the World: 365 Prayers, Poems and Invocations for Honouring the Earth*, Harper, San Francisco, 1991

Roberts, Jane *Seth Speaks: The Eternal Validity of the Soul. A Seth Book*, Amber-Allen Publishing, San Rafael, California, USA, 1994

——*The Individual and the Nature of Mass Events. A Seth Book*, Amber-Allen Publishing, San Rafael, California, USA, 1994

Roszak, Theodore, Mary E. Gomes and Allan D. Kanner *Ecopsychology – Restoring the Earth, Healing the Mind*, A Sierra Club Book, San Francisco, 1995

Roszak, Theodore *The Voice of the Earth: An Exploration of Ecopsychology*, Bantam Press, 1993

Shakespeare, William *Collected Works*, any edition

Schama, Simon *Landscape and Memory*, Harper Collins, London, 1995

Sheldrake, Rupert *The Rebirth of Nature: The Greening of Science and God*, Bantam Books, New York, 1991

Simpson, Ken and Nicolas Day *A Field Guide to Australian Birds*, Viking/Penguin, Australia, 1996

Small Wright, Machaelle *Behaving As If The God In All Things Mattered*, Perelandra, Jeffersonton, Virginia, USA, 1987

Tacey, David *Edge of the Sacred: Transformation in Australia*, Harper Collins Australia, 1995

Thoreau, Henry David *Walden* or *Life in the Woods*, any edition

——*The Portable Thoreau*, Carl Bode, editor, Viking Press, New York, 1947

Tompkins, Peter and Christopher Bird *Secrets of the Soil: New Age Solutions for Restoring Our Planet*, Harper and Row, New York, 1989

Wertheim, Margaret *Pythagoras' Trousers: God, Physics, and The Gender Wars*, Times Books, Random House, New York, 1995

Whitmont, Edward C. *The Return of the Goddess: Femininity,*

Aggression and the Modern Grail Quest, Routledge Kegan Paul, London, 1983

Wolf, Fred Alan *Parallel Universes: The Search for Other Worlds*, A Touchstone Book, Simon and Schuster, New York, 1990

Wolfe, Tom *The Bonfire of the Vanities*, Jonathan Cape, London, 1988

Wright, Judith *Going on Talking*, Butterfly Press, Springwood, NSW, Australia, 1992

Also from Bruce Sims Books

Zeno's Paradise
A novel by Bron Nicholls

Cornucopia City is divided against itself.

North of the river, the estuary is being poisoned and homeless children barely survive in deserted warehouses.

South of the river, the suburbs are green and pleasant. Martha Wellwright, radio talkshow host, lives with her family on the edge of a beautiful park. Zeno the Head Gardener has made a haven of order and tranquillity, where Martha's twin children are safe.

But nothing is as cleanly divided, or as safe, as it appears to be. The politics and economics of the late twentieth century catch up with Zeno's park, and the familiar routines of many people are disturbed: Pastor Ronny Hatchell, evangelist and developer; Maria and Vicente, illegal immigrants; Titania, director of the Midsummer Night's Dream company; half-mad Mervyn, inventor of *Realspace computer games. All, along with Martha's family and Zeno, find themselves staring into the heart of the Knowledge of Good and Evil.

Zeno's Paradise is a collision of many myths, old and new, which remind us how little we've changed when we are up against greed, jealousy and the desire for revenge; and love, of course.

Also from Bruce Sims Books

Heddy and Me
Susan Varga

'I notice, and not for the first time, that Mother glows when she talks of the war years, whereas her face fades and strains when we get to the present. Back then, the stage was large, and irrational forces dictated events. Now the wars are subtle and small and there never is a clear victory. Fighting your loved ones over well-worn territory. Fighting, in a way, over the outcome of those big years.'

Heddy and Me spans the twentieth century and some of its greatest upheavals: war, the holocaust, immigration.

In telling her mother's story, Susan Varga also tells her own. As a tiny baby she barely survived the holocaust, in hiding in a Hungarian village with her sister and her mother, Heddy. Neither the pain nor the devastation of this time lessened Heddy's will to go on and to recreate her life in Australia.

'... a seamless narrative. Varga's story of her mother and grandmother's life before and during the Nazi era is written with a classic simplicity and effortless flow ...' Mary Rose Liverani, *The Australian*

'This is a challenging, complex, rich, and above all, humane book. Into the process of creating it has gone great frankness and courage, and a hard-won recognition of the potential for destructiveness in the closest, most loving relationships.' Sara Dowse, *Canberra Times*

Also from Bruce Sims Books

Flight 642: Jakarta to Dili
An Australian journal
Jane Nicholls

In Jakarta, Jane Nicholls and her co-workers had to decide whether to flee or stay put in the terrifying breakdown of the rule of law before the repressive Soeharto regime fell.

Over a year later, living in a house that served as the office of the Fretilin Central Committee, she was admitted to the remarkable family of East Timorese, a people who were daring to hope that their freedom would come at last.

'Tonight we women talk about how it will be when the result of the ballot is known and the people have won. ''I will dance in the streets, and cry until I have no crying left.'' ''But Jane,'' says another, suddenly intensely serious, ''after the result of the ballot is known, and whether we win or lose, there will be a terrible massacre. Worse than 1975. We know that for certain and we are prepared.'' '

In her journal, Nicholls reflects on some of the complexities of Indonesia and East Timor. The actions of the military and the economic crisis are seen in human terms at ground level – the lives of people caught up in momentous national events, living in truly dangerous times. Its stage is the kitchen and the office as well as the streets of destruction and death.

It is the story of the everyday of history.

Bruce Sims Books are distributed by:

Australian Book Group

The distribution centre is care of Landmark Warehouse
PO Box 130, Drouin, Victoria 3818

Phone: 03 5625 4290

FAX: 03 5625 3756

Bookshops should enquire at these numbers to order or for
the contact details of their nearest sales representative.

Individual or bulk orders please contact the publisher.